FLOWER ON A LOWLY STALK
The Sixth Book of the Faerie Queene

FLOWER ON A LOWLY STALK

The Sixth Book of the Faerie Queene

by

ARNOLD WILLIAMS

MICHIGAN STATE UNIVERSITY PRESS

1967

CONTENTS

INTRODUCTION

THE SIXTH IS THE LAST complete book of the *Faerie Queene*. This is certainly one reason why it has been so little studied, but it cannot be the only reason. The fragment of two cantos commonly called the "Mutabilitie Cantos" which follows Book VI has received its share of attention, despite the impossibility of studying it in context. But studying any of Spenser's works in context, the ethical theme as embodied in the narrative pattern, the structure of the imagery as contributing to the ideological purpose, this has been extremely rare until quite recently, and even now is scarcely the dominant approach of criticism of the *Faerie Queene*.

As the last complete book of the *Faerie Queene*, Book VI deserves study in context and in depth. It is clearly Spenser's most mature work. Written after both the extreme rigidity of Book I and the extreme plasticity of Book III, it can profit from the defects of both extremes. Spenser's craftmanship is at its highest. He is still young, under fifty, and there is every evidence that he has mastered his form and that more fortunate things are to follow. The Mutabilitie Cantos are an indication of what was coming, but we cannot understand them as they deserve, because there is no context.

At the same time that Book VI is the last and most mature exercise of Spenser's poetic powers it is different from the other books. The virtue to which it is dedicated, courtesy, seems less exalted than the ones treated in the preceding books. Holiness, temperance, chastity, justice all outrank courtesy. It is perhaps equal to friendship, but of course that is not the real subject of Book IV. Spenser himself seems to agree with this hierarchy. He writes that the flower courtesy grows on a lowly stalk, yet none is fairer or spreads further abroad in "civility." By such a choice of images Spenser admits that courtesy is not necessary to heavenly salvation and perhaps not even to earthly well-being. It is not food or raiment, but ornament.

It is difficult to be sage and serious about courtesy, and Spenser is not. Courtesy is just not a heroic virtue, and from that fact comes almost all the distinction and charm of Book VI. The following pages will show, with almost monotonous regularity, how one after another of the usages usually considered specifically Spenserian are diminished or even absent. For instance, Spenser is still regarded as the most "allegorical" of English poets, yet this book has little of any of the various modes of communication miscellaneously heaped together as "allegory." Personification appears in only two minor episodes, mythology in two others. The incorporation of disguised history either of recent or remote events appears allusively in only a few stanzas of the final canto. Those nightmarish creatures like Maleger and Grandtorto have dwindled to the Blattant Beast. So with the benign supernatural; there is neither angel nor magic weapon in the whole length of the book.

Even some of the qualities of style imputed commonly to Spenser are hard to detect. Archaisms are few, as are also formal rhetorical schemes of ornament. For pages the Spenserian stanza seems to achieve the neutrality of blank verse.

From this inventory it would seem that what remains must be pale and tasteless. Perhaps it is to the sort of reader who finds *Samson Agonistes* uninteresting after *Paradise Lost*. But this sort of reader has been fooled by externals. It is true that Spenser's achieved control over his matter and his manner combines with the non-heroic theme to render unnecessary the more obvious externals of romance. The essence is still there: the multi-stranded narrative managed with consummate skill; the serious, even if unheroic theme, whose impact is rather enhanced than diminished by the frequent comic development; the fusing of narrative line and theme and image into a single whole. Almost all the characteristically Spenserian effects are here, but absorbed into the totality.

It will be part of the task of the ensuing study to break down this totality into its components. The more homogenous a literary work the greater hazard in analysis. Of necessity we have to take up one subject at a time. At least I have not been able to discover or devise a method of treating simultaneously the narrative line and pattern, the thematic meaning, and the imagistic structure, though manifestly these coexist. Each of the components of the finished work is like the famous school description of the location of the soul: whole in the whole and whole in every part. In part this study was first undertaken because I felt an incompleteness and misemphasis in studies which attacked only one of the components, whether it was theme or imagery or historical allusion. I have not seen any devoted solely to narrative; but they would probably be equally one-sided.

So I have chosen to analyze the whole book from end to end several times successively, once for the narrative line, once for the narrative pattern, once for the thematic line, and so on. Naturally, this procedure involves a good bit of repetition. The alternative procedure, commentary following the order of the narrative, would probably be more repetitious and less clear.

Students and colleagues have sometimes allowed me an approach to literature, but no one has ever accused me of having a theory or a philosophy of literature. The approach of the following pages is then eclectic.

I have sought to employ any technique or method which seemed to promise a deepening or a widening of the understanding of the Sixth Book of the *Faerie Queene*. The order of my inquiries is approximately: first the text itself, then the practice of chivalric romance, particularly by the Italians, and finally whatever I knew or could discover of the literary and philosophical ambience within which Spenser wrote. I have tried to bring all this to bear on the explication of the text; but from it to rear no generalized structure of theory, not even about the *Faerie Queene*.

Two virtually unsurmountable obstacles, which have seemed higher the nearer I approached, are terminology and documentation.

Literary critics and scholars, despite strenuous efforts by some of them, have been unable to achieve an agreed terminology which has the exactness enjoyed by their scientific colleagues. The obvious reason is that we do not deal with phenomena that can be quantified. Still, we could do better, for instance, with the term *allegory*. It must be apparent to anyone who reads criticism of the *Faerie Queene* that "allegory" covers several modes of writing which have little in common, except that they are not literal—and even that is a meaningless statement since no one can define "literal." I have tried to avoid the use of the word allegory except in quotes, indicating instead whether I mean personification, myth, or what not.

I cannot hope to have achieved such discrimination with certain other terms: theme, pattern, mode. When one reads in a respectable text that the fall of man is the "theme" of *Paradise Lost,* it seems hopeless to expect any agreement on the meaning of the term. In the following pages it always means an abstract, generalized statement of particular experience. At one stage in the writing I drew up a sort of glossary, with logical definitions of the principal terms. This device should have worked, but it didn't; the resultant writing might have passed for a treatise on metaphysics but it failed as criticism of imaginative literature. So I have fallen back on the good sense of the reader, who will I hope understand my terms in context.

I have been teaching the *Faerie Queene* and reading criticism and scholarship concerning it for three decades. In that time I must have absorbed a great many opinions and explanations of other scholars so thoroughly that I am no longer conscious of their origin. Many times I have written a preliminary sketch of the treatment of a particular episode, then gone to the library to read up on it, and found that one or more scholars had made the points I had made apparently independent of them. Was the point obvious? Or the independence illusory? Perhaps I read these articles or books when they came out fifteen or twenty years ago and the opinions had lodged in my mind.

I have tried to acknowledge my indebtedness in the commentary after the text, but I must have failed often. It has never been my practice to take notes when I read for general information.

One specific debt I am proud to acknowledge here, that to the *Annotated Bibliography of Edmund Spenser, 1937-1960* compiled by Waldo F. McNeir and Foster Provost and published in the Duquesne Studies. My own industry would never have provided such richness, especially the theses which have been so much help.

I

NARRATIVE

Narrative Line

THE NARRATIVE TECHNIQUE of Spenser's *Faerie Queene* is that of sixteenth century romance. Though his contributions to the totality of effect produced by the romance genre are many, and though he is highly original in the techniques of versification and the handling of theme, his innovations in narrative are inconsiderable, if they exist. He merely did with greater skill and for higher purposes what preceding writers of romance, both Italian and English, had already done.

The narrative technique characteristic of the long, and unfinished, romances of Boiardo and Ariosto, as well as the humbler prose ones like *Bevis of Hampton* and *Guy of Warwick*, derived from many sources, from märchen and epic, from Greco-Roman prose romance, from Eastern tale and Western exemplum. The important thing to understand about romance is that it is above all a way of telling a story. As such, it seems timeless. Some of the devices found in the earliest piece of narrative, the *Epic of Gilgamesh*, are still doing service in comic strips and television serials.

To whatever use, ethical, religious, political, the story material may be put, narrative structure is dictated by the requirements of telling a story, not by thematic purpose or the desire to explore personality. Typically, romance narrative is multi-stranded. It is not a filament, but a thread of many filaments. Some are longer, some shorter, they have varied colors, and the whole is composite. The polar opposite of romance narrative is the single line narrative, of which *Oedipus* is the greatest example, in which we follow one actor through a series of incidents which compose one action. Even in classical epic this singleness of narrative line prevails, though the number of incidents is naturally greater and the action longer.

Singleness is not desired in romance. In the simplest of the books of the *Faerie Queene*, the First, we have, after the first canto two lines of narrative running simultaneously, that of Redcross and that of Una. Starting out together the two characters are separated and the lines diverge, proceed in parallel fashion, and ultimately converge. We can visualize the process thus:

In the more complicated patterns of the later books, especially in Book VI, the lines bifurcate, the bifurcations bifurcate, and then converge to bifurcate anew:

You can visualize the development of a typical romance plot like that of Book VI of the *Faerie Queene* as a road map. This is an appropriate image, for romance narrative as practiced by Spenser is organized spatially rather than temporally. Characters move through space, their separations and junctures are at places. Perhaps the fact that the hero is on a quest produces this phenomenon; but it would be equally easy to argue that the desire to organize the narrative spatially generates the quest.

Whichever the cause, incidents are arranged according to space in the *Faerie Queene*. The character is typically pursuing or pursued, on a quest, a pilgrimage, a search. The hero rides up to a castle or encounters a friend or sees a villain oppressing an innocent maiden. The hero may spend a night at a castle, or stop to right an injustice, but always he resumes his journey. Despite Spenser's sometimes ornate references to time, fewer perhaps in Book VI than elsewhere, one inevitably thinks of a Spenser plot as a series of lines diverging and converging, crossing and bifurcating. The narrative analysis of such a plot inevitably produces something like a road map.

By the time Spenser has progressed as far as Book II, he is carrying these lines from one book to another. Apparently he occasionally forgot that he had not carried a line to its logical terminus, but such forgettings are infrequent, and he completes enough of the ones he has started to make us feel that, had he lived to complete the *Faerie Queene*, he might have completed virtually all of them. Guyon's sword and horse, lost in Book II, reappear in Book IV. Belphebe, first encountered in Book II, reenters the story in III, again in IV, and finally, by allusion, in Book VI. By the time Spenser had come to Book V, the practice of setting up at least one of the narrative lines of the succeeding book had become habitual. Book VI actually begins with the last canto of Book V. Previously, the quest has begun in Gloriana's court, where Redcross is given his commission to free Una's parents, Guyon to suppress Acrasia, Artegall to rescue Irena. But for the hunting of the Blattant Beast,* we step further back. We see the Beast in action before the complaint comes to Gloriana. Envy and Detraction set him on Artegall.

Besides serving a thematic purpose, this management of the narrative enables Spenser to build an entrance for Calidore, the quester of Book VI. The meeting of Calidore and Artegall, the ceremonial inauguration of the

---

* The reason for this spelling appears below, p. 67.

new knight by the old, is a narrative bridge to which the reader has become accustomed. The incident also naturally introduces the necessary exposition concerning the excellence of Calidore and the origins of the Blattant Beast. Learning that Artegall has seen the Beast, Calidore leaves him. Presently he comes on a squire tied to a tree.

So we proceed easily into the first episode of the book, the self-contained exemplum of Briana and Crudor. The squire supplies the necessary information: Briana, the lady of the nearby castle, has her servants cut the hair off ladies and the beards off knights who fall into their hands. From this hair she weaves a mantle to please her lover, Crudor. Calidore, the knight of courtesy, must of course rectify this discourteous custom. He fights his way inside the castle, kills the porter, and lectures Briana, who sends for Crudor. In the fight that follows, Calidore expectedly vanquishes Crudor, whom he forces to take Briana as his "loving fere." Briana, released of the necessity of proving her love for Crudor, ends the hair cutting and swears fealty to Calidore, who stays only long enough for his wounds to heal.

The Briana-Crudor episode is a sample of both theme and narrative. We have seen courtesy in action and so have a preview of the thematic contents of the book. We have Calidore's character fixed in our mind, though it is capable of greater development.

With the next episode we begin some continuing motifs and narrative lines. The story of Tristram and the Knight of the Barge* Spenser tells mostly in retrospect. As Calidore rides up, he sees a squire, Tristram, slaying a knight, the Knight of the Barge. In justification of the deed, Tristram tells what has happened. The locale of this and the next canto is a sort of fairyland equivalent of lovers' lane, a place where knights and ladies do their secret wooing, innocent of course. The Knight of the Barge, although provided with a lady of his own, breaks in on the privacy of a wooing couple, Aladine and Priscilla, tries to take Priscilla away from Aladine, wounds Aladine, and when Priscilla flees, takes out his frustration on his own lady by making her walk while he rides prodding her with his spear. We learn this from Tristram, whose account is authenticated by the lady of the dead knight.

Spenser is here handling at least two narrative lines, the self-contained story of the Knight of the Barge and Aladine-Priscilla and that of Tristram, a youth who wishes to attach himself to Calidore as a squire. The narrative encloses the enfance of Tristram, modelled on that of Percival

---

* I call him so because Aladine later identifies him as "bearing in his targe/A Ladie on rough waues, row'd in a sommer barge," (ii, 44). References to the *Faerie Queene* give the book, canto, and stanza. If no book is given, Book VI is understood. The text cited is that of the Variorum Spenser.

and utilizing the motif of the wicked uncle. Tristram cannot have his desire, for Calidore has taken a vow to achieve the quest of the Blattant Beast alone. A reader familiar with Spenser's narrative methods can be reasonably sure that, had Spenser written a book or two more of the *Faerie Queene*, we would have met Tristram again, just as Sir Satyrane, presented somewhat similarly in Book I, reappears in Books III and IV.

The episode of Aladine and Priscilla has no narrative continuation, that is the couple do not appear later in the book, but the motif of the interrupted couple is repeated, with variation and continuation, in the continuing story of Calepine and Serena. After making Tristram a squire and setting him to guard the lady of the Knight of the Barge, Calidore rides on to find Aladine wounded and Priscilla watching over him. This is the couple whose love making was interrupted by the Knight of the Barge, for the order of the presentation of events reverses the order of their occurrence.

Calidore and Priscilla carry Aladine home on Calidore's shield. Aladine's father, Aldus, receives him and we stop for an explanation of Priscilla's situation—her parents object to Aladine because they wish her to marry a great lord of the neighborhood—which motivates the ensuing action. The secret trysts of Aladine and Priscilla have exposed her to scandal. On reviving, Aladine's first thought is for Priscilla's reputation. Hence Calidore has to devise a way of justifying her plight to her parents. He returns to the scene of the previous episode, cuts off the head of the Knight of the Barge, and then conducts Priscilla home, where the sight of the head gives credence to Calidore's story that he rescued Priscilla from attack. Calidore, of course, omits any mention of Aladine.

Spenser is killing several birds with one stone. The story is a good exemplum of one application of courtesy. It also prepares, both thematically and narratively, for the following episode, Calepine and Serena. The initial situation here is identical to the one in Priscilla-Aladine: a young couple innocently wooing in a secret tryst. Calidore accidentally discovers them—Calidore instead of the Knight of the Barge, courtesy rather than discourtesy, accident instead of purpose. The result, however, is more grievous to the young couple than in the previous episode. For when Calidore offers an apology, Serena goes off a little way picking flowers to cover her embarrassment. Out of the forest rushes the Blattant Beast and carries Serena away. Calidore gives chase, the Beast drops Serena, who is injured by its poisonous fangs, and Calidore sets off in pursuit, leaving Calepine to care for Serena.

This is the last we see of Calidore for five and a half cantos. The whole middle of the book is devoted to several other lines of action: Calepine-Serena, which presently bifurcates; the punishment of the discourteous

6

knight Turpine, the Salvage* Man, Arthur, Timias. Through the whole middle of the book these lines arise, cross, combine and separate. In the total structure the adventures of Calidore frame these other stories.

As Calidore rides off in pursuit of the Beast, Calepine is trying to conduct the wounded Serena to safety. She rides his horse and he leads it. As night falls, they come to a river too deep for Calepine to wade. Turpine and his lady Blandina ride by on the other side. Calepine hails them to ask assistance, which Turpine, despite Blandina's entreaties, refuses. Calepine berates Turpine and challenges him, but Turpine only rides off, a hint of his cowardice to be developed subsequently. Calepine finds another crossing and comes to a castle, which is, of course, Turpine's. The porter refuses admission unless Calepine fights Turpine—this is the custom of the castle. Calepine protests his unpreparedness, Blandina again attempts in vain to mollify her lord, and Serena and Calepine spend the night outdoors, Calepine watching over the wounded Serena. In the morning the mounted Turpine attacks Calepine on foot and nearly kills him.

Calepine's desperate state sets up for the entrance of another character, the Salvage Man. This is the often-used motif of the rescue. Salvage chases Turpine away, then cares for Serena and Calepine. Spenser does not provide a biography for Salvage, as he so frequently does on the entrance of a new character; from hints in canto v, 1, the reader guesses that he is of noble blood, that his story will be told eventually, and that he is destined for further appearances. His function here is as a temporary protector of Serena and Calepine, and of Serena after Calepine wanders off and before the arrival of Arthur. After Arthur comes, Salvage remains in the story as his companion. Obviously, he is important to the theme.

In his role as protector, Salvage is able to cure Calepine's wounds by herbs; those of Serena are more stubborn. This difference in the effects of Salvage's treatment serves a narrative purpose as well as a thematic. Narratively, it sets up for the separation of Calepine and Serena. Recovered, Calepine goes out for a stroll. Seeing a bear with a babe in its mouth, he attacks the bear, forces it to release the babe, then kills it by stuffing a stone down its throat. The baby is unhurt, but Calepine must return it to its mother. He searches for hours before he finally comes on a woman lamenting.

She is Matilde, wife of Sir Bruin, who will lose his land unless he has an heir. Matilde has been unable to bear one, hence her lament. A prophecy has promised a son, who will "be gotten not begotten." Calepine fulfills the prophecy by giving the babe to Matilde. Sir Bruin apparently accepts the child as his natural heir.

* For the reason for this spelling, see below, p. 49.

Calepine and Serena are now separated, for he cannot find his way back to her. We resume the adventures of Serena, now linked to Salvage, who seeks Calepine without success. Serena's excessive grief starts her wounds bleeding again. Feeble as she is, she sets out in search of Calepine accompanied by Salvage, who carries Calepine's gear. Serena is still riding the horse, and when Salvage lays down the arms to repair Serena's saddle, Arthur and Timias come up.

Arthur has not appeared since Book V, canto xi, Timias not since Book IV, canto viii. Their introduction, therefore, requires some exposition. We are more concerned with Timias than with Arthur, whose role is the expected one of protector and avenger. Timias, however, is like Serena a victim of slander. Hence Spenser provides a flashback which brings up to date the story of the ever-rocky love affair between Belphebe and Timias. When we last heard of it in Book IV, its progress was for the moment smooth. But no sooner had Timias regained Belphebe's favor than new enemies, three personifications labelled Despetto, Defetto, and Decetto, tried to break up the affair. Failing, the three called in the Blattant Beast. Timias pursued it, overhauled it, and put it to flight, but in the chase was bitten.

In addition to updating the Timias-Belphebe story, obviously one of the main narrative lines of the whole work, Spenser has a parallel to the plight of Serena, reminds us of the Blattant Beast and Calidore's quest, and sets up for the thematic episode of the cure of Serena and Timias. We have noted how often Spenser uses the motif of separation and reunion. Thematically, slander is the cause of separation. Its cure will therefore establish the necessary condition for reunion. The reunion of Serena and Calepine comes a few cantos later; that of Timias and Belphebe is postponed beyond Book VI partly by the intervention of another separation motif in the Mirabella episode, partly by the narrative necessity of returning to the Calidore line. It is part of Spenser's grand design to keep the Timias-Belphebe line hanging just like the Arthur-Gloriana line.

At this point, the middle of Book VI, Spenser has created several lines of action. The pace of the narrative quickens with much cutting back and forth. Where before a whole canto was devoted to one line, now only a half a canto is so occupied. Calidore is pursuing the Blattant Beast; Turpine is yet unpunished for his discourtesy and cowardice; Calepine and Serena are separated; Serena and Timias suffer from the wounds of the Beast.

Spenser takes up the last of the lines first. Arthur, Serena, and Salvage come to a hermitage. The Hermit, who receives two biographies, one here and one in the next canto, takes over Arthur's responsibility for Serena and Timias. The Hermit cures the two, or rather, like a psychoanalyst, he shows them how they can cure themselves by avoiding the occasions of slander. A genealogy of the Blattant Beast reminds the reader of this line.

Soon after Serena and Timias leave the hermitage, they see the pageant of Mirabella, a fair lady riding a mangy jade led by a fool and a churl. Spenser merely initiates this motif, reserving it for later development.

When the Hermit undertook the cure of Timias and Serena, he released Arthur to pursue the punishment of the cowardly Turpine, a personage introduced previously in the Calepine-Serena episode. Seeking Turpine, Arthur and Salvage come to his castle and, since it is open, they enter. They tell the groom they are errant knights. When the groom becomes insulting, Salvage slays him. The retainers report the incident to Turpine, who upbraids Arthur and then, backed by forty retainers, attacks him and tries to strike him from behind. Arthur turns on Turpine and chases him to the bower of Blandina, who shields him. After Arthur contents himself with a lecture to Turpine, he leaves to assist Salvage in handling the forty retainers. He finds Salvage surrounded by a heap of bodies. The rest have fled. When Turpine reappears, Salvage attacks him, but is restrained by Arthur. Blandina entertains Arthur and by her arts somewhat mollifies him. When in the morning Arthur and Salvage leave, Turpine plans revenge.

His chance comes when two errant knights happen by looking for adventure and employment. By misrepresentation and offers of reward Turpine induces them to attack Arthur. They challenge him, one is killed, and the other, Sir Enias, tells Arthur they were deceived—apparently they expected an easy victory. As the price of his life Arthur requires Sir Enias to bring Turpine. This Enias does by leading Turpine to believe Arthur is slain. Arthur, however, is only sleeping, and Turpine soon perceives it. When Turpine turns on Enias with bitter words, Enias reminds him that he and his companion were likewise deceived by Turpine. Changing his approach Turpine then renews his suggestion that Enias kill Arthur: it will be easy while Arthur sleeps. Enias refuses, Salvage enters and, thinking the two menace Arthur, attacks them with a sapling he has uprooted. Arthur awakes, calls off Salvage, and seizes Turpine, now trembling with fright. As a proper punishment for his discourtesy and cowardice Arthur hangs Turpine up to a tree by the heels.

The Turpine line completed, Spenser cuts to Timias-Serena. At their last appearance, they were viewing the living tableau of Mirabella and her two persecutors, Disdain and Scorn. Then Spenser presented the scene only descriptively; now he provides the exposition which renders the scene meaningful. Mirabella is a fair but cruel lady who tortured her suitors. As penance Cupid has condemned her to wander accompanied by Disdain and Scorn, until she has saved as many loves as previously she lost.

9

Unlike some of the earlier tableaux, the procession of the seven deadly sins in Book I, canto iv, for instance, the Mirabella episode is integrated into the narrative development. The over-all narrative requires a separation of Timias and Serena so that Serena and Calepine can be reunited. Spenser uses Mirabella's plight as a means for producing this separation. Timias, angered at the treatment of Mirabella, tries to intervene. He is about to beat Scorn when his foot slips. Disdain, a powerful carl, pounces on Timias, puts a rope about his neck, and scourges him, while Scorn taunts him. Serena flees, and so Spenser has set up one of his favorite motifs, the fleeing maiden.

Leaving the Serena-Calepine line for later completion, Spenser stays with Timias-Mirabella. Arthur, Enias, and the Salvage Man ride up. Enias is first to attempt the rescue of Timias and Mirabella. Disdain knocks him down, Scorn is about to bind him, but Arthur slips under Disdain's guard and fells him. Arthur would kill Disdain, but Mirabella calls him off: her own life and welfare depend on Disdain. She explains her plight, Arthur releases Timias, and gives Disdain his freedom. Salvage attacks Scorn, Mirabella again intervenes. Mirabella must fulfill her penance and so Disdain and Scorn must remain with her.

Nearing the end of this middle section of the book, Spenser is closing out one after another of the lines of action he earlier initiated. Turpine has been left baffled, a satisfactory conclusion to an episode that is primarily comic. The end of the Mirabella episode marks the termination of the Arthur-Timias line, at least for this book. Serena and Calepine remain before Spenser can return to the main line of the book, Calidore's quest for the Blattant Beast.

The next episode then naturally opens with Serena's flight. She is mounted (the reader may have forgotten the horse which appears first in canto iii, but Spenser has not) and covers a good bit of territory. When all is apparently safe, she dismounts and delivers a complaint about her miserable plight, alone and helpless. She blames chiefly Calepine, who, she thinks, deserted her. This is a device to remind the reader of Calepine, absent from the action for four cantos and about to reenter it. There is also an element of contrast, for we presently learn that Calepine has been seeking Serena, and he finds her just in time.

After her complaint the exhausted Serena sleeps. A marauding band of cannibals come up and capture Serena. They briefly debate what to do with her and decide to sacrifice her to their god. When she wakes they strip her. Serena's beauty, described in one of Spenser's most sensuous passages, stirs lust in the Cannibals. The priest, however, restrains them and holds them to their duty. The ceremony begins, Serena nude and tied to an altar, the Cannibals raising a din of bagpipes, horns, and cries.

By the coincidence conventional to romance, Calepine is nearby and, hearing the noise, comes to investigate. The knife in the priest's hand is about to lance Serena's breast. Calepine rushes into the throng and, aided by the darkness and the confusion, kills "swarms" of the Cannibals and puts the rest to flight. Serena, ashamed of her nudity, will not speak to Calepine until the morn discovers her condition. Spenser quickly ends the episode with a promise of further development—a promise we must suppose he would have kept in a subsequent book.

All the secondary lines have now come to their end. Spenser's narrative practice does not demand that all lines converge at the end of a book, as for instance, the lines of a play must converge at the end. Actually, he leaves several lines hanging, satisfactorily ended for the narrative and thematic purposes of Book VI, but not intrinsically complete: Arthur, Timias-Belphebe, Serena-Calepine, possibly Mirabella. The last can stand as complete, but there is no reason why Spenser should not have returned to Mirabella for further development.

Calidore left the action in canto iii, pursuing the Blattant Beast. When he reenters at the opening of canto ix, he is still pursuing it. He has chased the Beast from court to city, to town, to settled country, to remoter areas on the fringe of civilization, when he comes on a community of Shepherds. Here in Arcady* the quest is suspended while Calidore enjoys the innocent life of Melibee and woos Melibee's supposed daughter, the shepherdess Pastorella.

Though Calidore seemingly forgets his duty and though the rapid narrative of adventure slows down to the pace of pastoral ease, the episode is not a digression. Thematically, Calidore's experiences parallel those of Redcross at the House of Holiness. They are really preparation for success in his quest. Much of the material, the praise of the golden age as exemplified by the shepherds of Arcady and Calidore's sight of the dancing maidens on Mount Acidale, is rather more thematic than narrative. The situation, however, generates another narrative development, with the familiar branching of lines.

Besides Calidore, the chief actors are Melibee, Pastorella, Coridon, the Brigands, Bellamoure and Claribell. After Calidore has won Pastorella's love from his rustic rival, Coridon, he sees Colin Clout playing to the dancing ring of naked maidens, and then, when they vanish, rescues Pastorella from a tiger. Calidore's heroism—his only weapon is a sheep hook—is perhaps narrative preparation for the more desperate rescue which will follow.

While Calidore is out hunting and so separated from Pastorella, a band of Brigands on a slave raid attacks the shepherds, pillages their homes, and captures the whole population, Melibee, Coridon, and Pastorella included.

---

* Spenser gives no specific name to the place. For ease of reference I call it Arcady.

The merchants who come to buy slaves insist that Pastorella be included in the lot, else they will not buy any. The captain of the Brigands, however, lusts for Pastorella and will not sell her. Fearing worse, she has temporized by encouraging his attentions. So he fights the other Brigands in a typically Spenserian melee. The captain defends himself and Pastorella until he is killed and she wounded in the arm. The surviving Brigands sort out the living from the dead, find Pastorella still alive, and revive her. They leave her in charge of one of her number, who tries to molest her.

When Calidore returns, he finds Melibee's hut wrecked, Pastorella and all the shepherds gone. Coridon, who has escaped, returns to tell Calidore what has happened. After venting his grief, Calidore promises to reward Coridon for leading him to the Brigands' island. The two find the Brigands watching the sheep they have stolen and so hire themselves out as shepherds. That night Calidore reconnoiters the caves and locates Pastorella. He breaks in the cave where she is imprisoned, slays the guard, and then kills the other Brigands as they enter. Leaving all the spoils to Coridon, Calidore departs with Pastorella.

Spenser again uses the separation motif, but this time not as an introduction to disaster, but for a reunion. Calidore remembers his quest of the Blattant Beast, leaves Pastorella at the castle of Belgard in the care of Sir Bellamoure and Lady Claribell. An expository flashback tells us their story, a partial repetition of the motif of the Priscilla-Aladine episode. Bellamoure loved Claribell against the opposition of her parents. When her father discovered their secret marriage, he imprisoned both of them. Bellamoure, however, found means of access to Claribell and begot a daughter. When born, the child was given to a servant, who abandoned it where Melibee found and adopted it. As any reader of romance would expect, Pastorella is the missing daughter, who, after the servant recognizes the birthmark, is reunited with her parents.

Here Spenser leaves the line of Pastorella to resume that of Calidore. His pursuit of the Blattant Beast among the clergy, where it ruins churches and monasteries, leads to an eventual baying of the Beast. After a struggle in which the Beast relies more on its tongue than its fangs, Calidore subdues and muzzles it. He leads it through Fairyland and it remains chained for a long time. With a brief account of its later history —it breaks loose again—Spenser closes Book VI and, though not intentionally, the *Faerie Queene*.

The two narrative lines developed in the last section of the book are obviously not brought to convergence. One expects the affair of Calidore and Pastorella to reach a conclusion, if not in marriage, at least in betrothal, as with Redcross and Una. Only a modest faith in Spenser's narrative skill is required to suppose that he would have concluded the

Calidore-Pastorella love in Book VII or later, probably also that of Calepine and Serena. The Arthur-Gloriana and Timias-Belphebe lines he
would certainly have kept going until the very end of the work. What he
would have done with Tristram and the Salvage Man is beyond conjec-
ture. That he would not have left so many loose ends receives confirma-
tion from Spenser's previous practice. Book II, for instance, is thematically complete, and so is its main narrative line, Guyon's quest, but many
lines initiated in it are continued and developed in later books: Belphebe,
Guyon's sword and horse, and Bragaddochio. Book III is in no sense
completed, even with the ending of the 1590 version. Most of the loose
ends are, however, tied in by the end of Book IV. Book V is rather self-
contained, like Book I, with the exception of the Blattant Beast, an obvious set up for Book VI. What more natural than for Spenser in Book VI
to return to the pattern of Book III? Leaving a number of loose ends at
the end of the second installment of the *Faerie Queene* has the same
virtue as leaving them at the end of the first installment: it entices readers
to buy the next installment, if for no other reason, to see how the stories
come out.

These must, of course, remain unverifiable guesses. The burning of
Kilcolman and the ensuing untimely death of Spenser make them so.

Pattern

A REVIEW of the narrative line shows the narrative in motion. Incidents follow one another in the order in which Spenser placed them, each connected only with what precedes and what follows. It is also valuable to see the incidents abstracted from their surroundings. When so viewed, incidents will be seen to have other connections, other orders will emerge, and a design, still narrative but not dependent on the narrative line, will become visible. For instance, in the narrative line the rescue of Pastorella is connected with her capture by the Brigands and with her reunion to her parents. But if we abstract it from the line, we see that in some ways, but not all, it duplicates the rescue of Serena by Calepine. This sort of connection, we may call, for the sake of having a term, narrative pattern.

In analyzing narrative patterns in Book VI, we naturally begin with the abstract relationship of incident to line. A specific incident can either be part of the line, continuing what preceded and preparing for what follows; or it can be expository, past action narrated to explain present action. Like a dramatist of the Ibsen school who must tell his story without a prologue or a chorus, Spenser usually begins an episode, even a whole narrative line, with an action, which may continue some time before we know who the actors are and why they act so. Then we get the explanation, which is often the biography of the personage entering the story or, if we are picking up a narrative line from a previous section of the *Faerie Queene,* an account of a personage's fortunes since we last met him.

Thus, when Calidore first meets Aladine and Priscilla, the narrative only concerns how Aladine, for some time unnamed, met his mishap, Priscilla's concern about him, Calidore's attempts to help the two lovers. It is only after Calidore and Priscilla have taken Aladine to his home, that we get the necessary expository material which explains why they were in the secret trysting place where the Knight of the Barge found them. Priscilla and Aladine had to meet secretly because her parents opposed the match, preferring a neighboring lord of greater power and riches. We have not needed this information to understand the action up to the time when Priscilla begins to worry about her reputation and Calidore undertakes the delicate mission of conducting her home without telling her parents the whole story of her misfortunes.

Likewise, when Arthur and Timias ride into the story, we have to be filled in on what has happened between Timias and Belphebe since we last met them in Book IV. Timias is suffering from the bite of the Blattant Beast and we have to know how he was bitten. The Priscilla-Aladine line can proceed some distance before the exposition becomes necessary; we need that concerning Timias-Belphebe at once. Most often, Spenser provides his exposition at the point where it is necessary to understand the story, and generally speaking, he is adept in introducing his exposition. Most of it is enclosed narrative, a sort of flashback, around which the narrative line flows. Sometimes these enclosed narratives come early, as with Timias, sometimes later as with Priscilla.

A characteristic sample is the enclosed narrative of Matilde and Sir Bruin in canto iv. Calepine has rescued a baby from a bear and is looking for the parents. He finds no one until he comes on a woman mourning. When Calepine sympathetically suggests that she can relieve her grief by sharing it with him, she tells the story of her husband, Sir Bruin, who has conquered the land from a giant, Cormorant, but will lose it unless he has an heir, which Matilde has been unable to provide. The prophecy that a son will "be gotten not begotten" brings the enclosed narrative into connection with the Calepine line, for he naturally fulfills the prophecy by giving the baby to Matilde. The enclosed narrative thus explains Matilde's grief, relates Calepine's action to the theme of the book, and produces the separation of Calepine and Serena, for by the time all the requirements of politeness have been met, Calepine cannot find her.

Quite different from the enclosed narrative is the self-contained one. This can be illustrated by the first action of Book VI, the Briana-Crudor episode. This falls in the main line of narrative, and since Calidore is the Champion of Courtesy it is also an exemplum of courtesy. But the episode stands alone narratively. It has neither precedent nor continuation. Briana and Crudor appear in it and then drop out of the story. Nor is the motif of the hair cutting used in subsequent narrative as preparation, repetition, or parallel. The episode could stand alone. If the whole book were composed of such episodes it would be like a string of beads.

Spenser frequently opens a book with such a self-contained episode. Book I begins with Redcross' slaying the Dragon of Error; the Amavia-Mortdaunt-Ruddymane episode that opens Book II is not self-contained, since it motivates the quest; but the next following episode, Guyon's entertainment at the house of Elissa, Perissa, and Mediana is self-contained, though personification-allegory, instead of romance narrative. In Book V the exemplum of Sanglier and Artegall's judgment of Solomon is a precise parallel to the Briana-Crudor episode.

If Spenser often begins a book with a self-contained episode, he as often follows with one that begets a narrative line. The slaying of Error is followed immediately by the stop at Archimago's hermitage; and as soon as Calidore recovers from the wounds he sustained at Briana's castle he moves on into the Knight of the Barge incident. We would call this self-contained, for none of the characters, except Calidore, reappear in Book VI. However, it is pretty clear that Tristram will reappear in a later book, and Spenser is setting up a narrative line for subsequent use. Moreover, the Priscilla-Aladine episode, even within the pattern of Book VI, is repeated with variations in Serena-Calepine, which becomes a narrative line.

The narrative of the whole of canto ii and the first nineteen stanzas of canto iii illustrates still another pattern, which we may call interrupted, or interwoven. There are actually two connected stories: the attack on Priscilla and Aladine and Tristram's killing of the Knight of the Barge. From the point of view of chronology, the incidents are narrated in reverse order. The Knight of the Barge beat Aladine and frightened Priscilla before Tristram killed him. Here the space order prevails over the time. Calidore comes to the one scene before he reaches the other, just a traveller proceeding southwest would see the results of a tornado blowing northeast in the reverse order of their occurrence.

The interruption comes in the circumstance that we learn of the attack on Priscilla and Aladine (unnamed at this point) and then become concerned with other matters: the behavior of the Knight of the Barge after the attack (stanzas 21-22), which led to Tristram's intervention (23), the enclosed enfance of Tristram (24-33), Calidore's making Tristram a squire and entrusting the lady to him (37-40). Then we return to Priscilla and Aladine, whom Calidore now discovers. The time pattern is identical with that of *Oedipus*, where successive disclosures go ever backward in time, but here backward flowing time is forward flowing space.

The handling of the Priscilla-Aladine episode is also a miniature of the pattern followed in the central part of the book. Here Spenser keeps two, three, or four lines of narrative going at one time, with interruptions, cutting back and forth, and numerous enclosures for exposition. Spenser's narrative pattern is thus similar to Shakespeare's dramatic one.* In the early parts of a book Spenser tends to pursue one line for a canto or more; as the lines become more numerous and the pace of the narrative speeds up, he may take up two lines in one canto (e.g., in canto vi), occasionally even three, as in canto vii. In Book VI the number of narrative lines increases, and consequently the amount of space given each block decreases, from canto iii through canto viii. Canto ix is given wholly to one line, Calidore-Pastorella, which then divides in canto x, the parts rejoining at the end of canto xi and redividing in canto xii, never to rejoin.

---

* It was not of course invented by Elizabethans. It is found full blown in fifteenth century drama, both in the cycle plays and in such miracle plays as *Mary Magdalen*. The dramatists may well have borrowed it from cyclical Arthurian romance.

The tempo of the book therefore increases up to the end of canto viii, slows down decidedly in canto ix, then increases again, but never reaches the acceleration it had attained in canto viii. Spenser does not return at the end of Book VI to the slow tempo with which it started, as he does in I, II, and IV. This is probably a sign of intended continuation, for we notice the same phenomenon at the end of III and V. Another way of putting it is that I and II are relatively self-contained, Books III and IV go together to make a two book unit. But for the Blattant Beast episode, which may be an afterthought, Book V would be a unit like I and II. Both the tempo of the last two cantos and the absence of another narrative line suggest that Spenser was returning to the one book unit. With Book VI he is certainly repeating the two book unit—or perhaps even he planned a three book one.

There is, then, a rough correlation between number of narrative lines, tempo, and size of unit (whether one or two books). In making such a statement I emphasize the word *rough*. Spenser is not as schematic a poet as was Dante; the conditions of his work made for interruptions and consequent forgetfullness of small details;* and his natural inventiveness and variety sometimes obscure the narrative pattern beneath. Nevertheless, once we reduce the incidents to narrative lines we will see in every book of the *Faerie Queene* a general practice of a slow start, increasing tempo coincident to the increase of narrative lines, a slowing tempo in the last third or fourth of the book, and then an increasing tempo in the last canto or two, coming to a quick close.

The relation of tempo to clock time is an interesting one. From the point of view of narrative, as distinguished from various affective devices, such as versification, tempo is not so much a matter of time as of place. This flows from the nature of romance, in which action is conceived as more spatial than temporal. More strictly phrased, the space-time continuum is presented as space rather than time. To see the implications for narrative of this practice, one has only to contrast any romance with most novels of the last two centuries, or even better with the representational drama, as written by Ibsen, where there is often no change of scene at all, and the only order the author can give to events is a temporal one.

Most of the main personages in the *Faerie Queene* are homeless, the vicious ones as well as the virtuous one, both Redcross and Duessa. They are always going from somewhere to somewhere, stopping only temporarily. We rarely see them either at the starting point or the terminus of their journey. The champions are on a quest. Many of the lesser personages are also seeking something: e.g., the Squire of Dames is searching for a virtuous woman. Many of the women are being pursued, and some-

---

* For instance, the confusion between Guyon and Redcross in III, ii, 4-16.

times the pursuer is in turn pursued, as in the chase after Florimell. Tempo, then is a combination of how much ground the personages cover and how much the reader covers shifting from one line of action to another. Spenser can speed up the tempo by "short cutting," that is, by frequent shifts from one narrative line to another, or he can slow it down by shifting from one line in which the personages are in rapid motion to another in which they are proceeding at a leisurely pace. This is exactly what happens when he closes out the Serena-Calepine line at the end of canto viii and shifts to Calidore.

Minor characters like Briana, the Hermit, and Turpine have local habitations. Melibee and Pastorella live in a shepherd's cottage in Arcady until they get absorbed into the story. Then they are carried away from their home by the Brigands, Melibee to die and Pastorella to be deposited with Bellamoure and Claribell. Here we have two different uses of place. For Pastorella it is a point of departure, but for Briana, the Hermit, and Turpine it is permanently associated with their character. The story passes through and picks up Pastorella; it merely passes through Briana's castle.

Throughout the *Faerie Queene* we encounter castles, houses, hermitages, caves, even streams and strands, each inhabited by a character or set of characters. The pattern of constant motion then combines with a pattern of fixed habitation, with a differentiation between personages according to whether they are moving or remain fixed. This combination of patterns is characteristic of the Arthurian cyclical romance, but it is also even more characteristic of another literary form, the drama. Except for the English cycle plays, all medieval drama is built on a station-and-place arrangement of the playing space. A glance at such a play as the *Castle of Perseverance* will make this plain. God, World, Flesh, Devil, and Couvetousness have stations or scaffolds assigned to them, as do also the seven virtues. Mankind and six of the deadly sins move from one station to another through the neutral space between and around the stations.

The questions which came first, the romance or the dramatic use of space and place, and how much Spenser derived from each practice are primarily historical and of no great concern for the critical understanding of the pattern of the *Faerie Queene*. It is enough to recognize that, for thematic reasons, Spenser adopted something like the station and place arrangement of the drama. He can then set up contrasts between places, the House of Pride and the House of Holiness in Book I, which are also contrasts between moral positions, and by having Redcross stop at both houses Spenser works out his spiritual progress in terms of space. This practice is what lies behind the homeless champion proceeding from one fixed place to another. In Book VI less thematic meaning attaches to the fixed places than elsewhere in the *Faerie Queene* for reasons which we will fully explore later.

If then we think of homeless characters moving through unlocalized space to a series of fixed places, each place separated from another by an unspecified length of space, we have a clue to the presence or absence of temporal references. Beyond such vague formulas "One day as he did range the fields abroad," (x, 5), you will not find many temporal references when personages are in space. For instance, when Disdain and Scorn capture Timias, Serena flees the scene. She is therefore freed from place and free in space, and appropriately Spenser does not tell us how long she fled, but how far: "Through hils and dales, through brushes and through breres," (viii, 32), until she thought she had put enough distance behind her to dismount in safety. She has, of course, come to another part of fairyland, another place, if you will, where there are cannibals, and with the shift of scene we are ready for a new episode.

Temporal references are necessary when a personage stops at a place. Night and day may be especially important. Both rescues, of Serena by Calepine and of Pastorella by Calidore, have to take place at night, because the outnumbered champions need darkness as an ally. When a character stops at a place, temporal references may also be necessary, since the usual spatial order for events is lacking. But Spenser rarely needs any temporal unit larger than day and night. He has a habit of collapsing time, as, for instance, when he passes over Calidore's stay at Briana's castle to allow his wounds to heal. He takes three lines for a period of time which could hardly be less than three weeks:

> There he remaind with them right well agreed,
> Till of his wounds he wexed whole and strong,
> And then to his first quest he passed forth along. (i, 47)

On the other hand, the one night Arthur spent at Turpine's castle (vi, 41-44) requires three stanzas, because it has the important narrative function of setting up for Turpine's treachery in the following canto.

The only apparent exception to the rule that Spenser's principal characters are in constant motion from place to place is Calidore's stay in Arcady. This is a definite place, not a castle or a hermitage, but still localized space. Calidore does almost nothing while there: he helps Pastorella with the sheep and woos her. Nevertheless, if the episode is to serve its narrative and thematic purpose, it must take up sufficient of the reader's time not to seem a trivial incident. Spenser solves the problem by introducing two passages dominantly reflective rather than narrative: Melibee's discourse on the Golden Age (ix, 20-36) and the vision on Mount Acidale, (x, 5-31). Though satisfactory as a solution, this seems not entirely to have satisfied Spenser the narrator, for he also included one incident of rapid action, the tiger's attack on Pastorella. This is not a very happy invention, more interruptive than contributory, though there is perhaps another reason for its inclusion.

The method of introducing new personages into the narrative line depends partly on whether they are at rest or in motion. The point of view of the narrative presentation, whether omniscient or limited, is also partly determined by this dichotomy between motion and rest. Modern critics of fiction have shown that the older classification of points of view into first person (limited) and third person (omniscient) is over simplified, and that a range of intermediate possibilities lies between these two extremes. Modern writers of fiction, generally pledged to a limited point of view in which they can narrate only what an actual human being could see, hear, or know, have nevertheless found the need of omniscience, and so have created all sorts of devices, the "camera eye" of Dos Passos, for instance, to achieve greater universality than a limited point of view permits. Showing sometimes has to be supplemented by telling.

The problems of point of view and the choice between telling and showing are pertinent to narrative at all times. The practice of Spenser shows his awareness of them and his efforts to deal with them. In general, he preferred showing to telling, and his point of view, though third person, is often quite limited. Except for occasional exercises of omniscience to give a hint of real meaning and eventual outcome, as when he describes Archimago "sober he *seemde,* and very sagely sad," Spenser prefers most of the time to stick to things visible and audible to a skillful spectator not too far from the action. Commentary Spenser practices, and first person interjections as well as a variety of other practices not wholly consonant with the limited observer. But these are mostly confined to thematic sections, to narrative bridges, and to enclosed expository material. Moreover, these sections are usually marked off distinctly from the main narrative. The dominant point of view is then limited, and the dominant method of presentation showing rather than telling.

The severest test of the maintenance of a limited point of view comes when new personages enter the narrative. If these are at rest, there is usually no problem. The management of the first episode, Briana's castle, illustrates the usual process. Calidore comes to a squire tied to a tree. Calidore naturally asks the squire how he got in this predicament, and the squire as naturally tells his story, during the course of which we meet Briana:

> The Lady which doth owne
> This Castle, is by name *Briana* hight. (i, 14)

and in the next stanza, her lover, Crudor, and her seneschal, Maleffort. Later, as a result of this information, Calidore storms Briana's castle, and we meet the lady in person. In somewhat similar fashion Spenser introduces Turpine, the Hermit, Melibee, and Pastorella into the story.

When personages are in motion, the process of introduction has to be somewhat different, and the maintenance of the point of view may be more difficult. We often meet the personage performing some action: Calidore first sees Tristram from a distance. Tristram is fighting a knight and, before Calidore comes up, slays him. Spenser describes the scene as Calidore would see it, not as the omniscient author sees it. Neither Tristram nor the slain knight is immediately identified. For Tristram the lack is soon remedied. Answering Calidore's questions, he introduces himself and gives Calidore (and us) an extensive enfance: "And Tristram is my name, the onely heire / Of good King *Meliogras*" (ii, 28). Matilde similarly introduces herself to Calepine; "I am th' vnfortunate Matilde by name / The wife of bold Sir *Bruin.*"

But sometimes the action is proceeding so rapidly, or the introduced personages are in such straits, that Spenser cannot follow the method of self introduction. Priscilla and Aladine are in no shape to identify themselves, much less to give Calidore an extensive vita. Calidore is in the position of a highway patrolman who must take care of the victims and get the wrecked cars off the road before he can get names and addresses and details of the accident. The same difficulty attends the entrance of Mirabella. Presumably, Arthur, Timias, and Serena cannot get close enough to her, guarded as she is by Disdain and Scorn, to get these details.

The two episodes illustrate two different solutions. The Aladine-Priscilla incident is a model of good technique, if one accepts the standards on which Ibsen insisted in drama and Henry James in fiction. There is no detail which could not be known to an observer located a few paces behind Calidore. The order of presentation is thoroughly that of the observer, for as we have noted it reverses the order of happening.

But the management of the incident is not happy; it proves that the avoidance of omniscience carries its own perils. We first meet Tristram, the Knight of the Barge, and his lady early in canto ii (stanza 3). Tristram identifies himself in stanza 28, but we never learn the name of either the slain knight or his lady. We learn of the attack on Priscilla and Aladine in stanza 16 and actually meet the couple in stanza 41, yet no names appear until canto iii, stanza 3 for Aladine and stanza 10 for Priscilla. In describing the attack on Priscilla and Aladine, Spenser has to handle four characters, none of them named.

The awkwardness and confusion that result, compounded by Spenser's

notorious looseness in pronoun reference, become visible when we repro-
duce the narrative with the references bracketed in:

In which she [Lady of the Knight of the Barge] shew'd, how that discourteous
  knight [of the Barge]
(Whom *Tristram* slew) them [Priscilla and Aladine] in that shadow found,
Ioying together in vnblam'd delight,
And him [Aladine] vnarm'd, as now he [Aladine] lay on ground,
Charg'd with his [Barge's] speare and mortally did wound,
Withouten cause, but onley her [Priscilla] to reaue
From him [Aladine], to whom she [Priscilla] was for euer bound,
Yet when she [Priscilla] fled into that couert greaue
He [Barge] her [Priscilla] not finding, both them [Priscilla and Aladine] thus
  nigh dead did leaue. (ii, 43)

At least once more in Book VI Spenser delays his exposition too long.
Sir Enias appears first in canto vii, 3, as one of two unnamed free lance
knights deceived by Turpine into attacking Arthur. One of the two is
killed in the ensuing fight, but the other, Sir Enias, stays in the story,
nameless and referred to only by periphrases, "that same knight," "the
gentle knight," "that other knight," until Turpine is baffled. Then
Spenser shifts to the Mirabella line for the remainder of the canto, and it
is not until stanza 4 of the following canto viii that we learn Sir Enias'
name:

> They met Prince *Arthur* with Sir *Enias*
> (That was that courteous knight, whom he before
> Hauing subdew'd, yet did to life restore).

The confusion is not as great as in the Priscilla-Aladine episode, for
after canto vii, stanza 9 Sir Enias is the only unnamed character in the
action. Still, it leads Spenser into many awkward periphrases. And in the
end he still presents the information omnisciently, so his only gain is that
it is presented at a time when Arthur could have learned it naturally.

These two samples of the difficulties of a too restricted point of view
are ample to justify Spenser's frequent abandonment of it in favor of
omniscience. The Mirabella episode is much smoother because after
showing us the pageant of Mirabella riding her mangy jade Spenser omnisciently intervenes to tell us the whole story of her plight in an enclosed
expository narration. In several other places he solves the problem of
identity of newly introduced characters by Horatio Alger's favorite
formula, "Tom Thatcher, for this was our hero's name": "Fair Mirabella
was her name"; "the fair Serena (so his lady hight)"; "Sir Calepine (so
hight)."

What we have examined are patterns for variety, complexity, and excitement. They are mostly centrifugal. If there were no corresponding unifying patterns, Spenser's narrative would quickly become disorganized and chaotic. Even the unity given by theme—the illustration of courtesy in Book VI—would not save the narrative from flying off in all directions. At the least, the *Faerie Queene* would be what Boiardo's *Orlando Innamorato* and Ariosto's *Orlando furioso* are, not only incomplete, but also incompletable.

The larger the number of narrative lines, the more numerous the characters, the more varied the incidents, the greater is the risk of disorganization, and the more pressing the need of centripetal patterns to balance the centrifugal.

What methods does Spenser use to keep his narrative lines parallel instead of divergent and to make them converge when they must? We have noted that he uses two methods to introduce and identify new characters: intrinsic patterns that grow out of the narrative itself (the porter tells Calepine that the lord of the castle in which he seeks shelter is named Turpine); and extrinsic, the intervention of the omniscient author. This dichotomy will also serve as well for the analysis of methods to unify a multiplex narrative.

The extrinsic patterns are the easier to analyze, because, being somewhat outside the narrative, they are obvious. Spenser uses a variety of these. The most apparent is the connection of theme with narrative in the essay material with which he often opens a canto. The first three stanzas of canto ii provide an illustration. The first stanza begins with the question:

> What vertue is so fitting for a knight,
> Or for a Ladie, whom a knight should loue,
> As Curtesie, to beare themselues aright
> To all of each degree, as doth behoue?

This is pure commentary on the nature and value of courtesy, which Spenser then expands: courtesy has to do with the proper relationships between persons, regardless of their class: "Whether they be placed high aboue, / Or low beneath." Just because you have power and position, you cannot throw your weight around.

The second stanza elaborates further. Courtesy, especially the proper treatment of inferiors, comes naturally to some people, "some so goodly gratious are by kind," whereas others, with better intellectual gifts have to work hard and still do not attain in every thing the courtesy of the naturally favored; yet they deserve praise for their sincere efforts.

What has this to do with the story? The next stanza answers the question: "That well in courteous *Calidore* appeares." After a brief, abstract description of Calidore's courtesy Spenser turns to the narrative: "He now againe is on his former way" to pursue his quest of the Blattant Beast. Before the end of the stanza Calidore sees a youth fighting a knight. This, of course, makes concrete the remarks about social position. A contest between an experienced knight on horse and an untrained youth on foot is a violation of courtesy. In fact, the whole succeeding narrative exemplifies in the exploits of the Knight of the Barge the evil of taking advantage of superior power. The proper use of superiority, as Calidore demonstrates, is to help instead of to abuse inferiors. So the thematic essay has really been an abstract of the narrative.

Not counting the proem or the first canto, seven of the eleven cantos of Book VI begin with an essay like this, which, within three stanzas, is applied to the following narrative. The essays thus forecast the succeeding story thematically, as the introductory quatrains forecast it narratively.

In canto iv the Salvage Man rescues Calepine from Turpine and cares for Calepine and Serena. Canto v begins with a statement that gentle blood will produce gentle deeds, regardless of environment. Spenser is abstracting the meaning of the Salvage Man's deeds in rescuing Calepine, but also preparing for Salvage's protection of Serena, soon to be separated from Calepine. Serena's malady is beyond Salvage's cure; hence canto iv opens with an essay on the effects of calumny, which are worse than the wounds of a sword, because no leach can cure them, a forecast of the Hermit's prescription to Serena and Timias.

Four cantos open, not with essays, but with narrative summaries. Of course, every canto of the *Faerie Queene* has a quatrain of argument prefixed, but these are all prospective, what is to happen. These four narrative summaries are retrospective and bridging, some of them marking shifts in the narrative line from the preceding canto. Canto iii closes with Calepine and Serena refused shelter by Turpine because Calepine is neither physically able to fight Turpine nor willing to jeopardize Serena's safety. Despite their condition, Serena suffering from the bite of the Beast and Calepine from Turpine's beating, they spend the night in the open. Calepine is torn with anxiety for Serena and resentment against Turpine. Spenser thus opens canto iv with a simile comparing Calepine's state to a storm-tossed ship.

> Like as a ship with dreadfull storm long tost,
> Hauing spent all her mastes and her ground-hold,
> Now farre from harbour likely to be lost. . . .

This is retrospective; the next lines are prospective:

At last some fisher barke doth neare behold.

The first action of the canto is the appearance of the Salvage Man who scares off Turpine and cares for the helpless couple.

Canto ix, which picks up the Calidore line dropped five cantos earlier, also begins with a narrative summary incorporated in a simile, this time of the plowman who has left some furrows unplowed:

> Now turne again my teme, thou iolly swain,
> Backe to the furrow which I lately left.

The unplowed furrow is Calidore's quest. The direct address fades into a rapid summary of Calidore's pursuit of the Beast, which finally brings him to Arcady and Pastorella. Having been a furrow in canto ix, Calidore's quest becomes a ship in the opening of canto xii, a ship fighting contrary winds that threaten to blow it off course, yet making way.

Only one of the four narrative summaries that open cantos is non-figurative, the one at the beginning of canto x, which asks the question, "Who now does follow the foule *Blatant Beast?*" Not Calidore, for he follows "that faire Mayd / Vnmyndfull of his vow." This is, however, not quite a literal statement, for it probably contains some irony. Thematically at least, the episode in Arcady particularly the sight of the dancing graces on Mount Acidale, is not digressive, but preparatory.

We have noted that the number of narrative lines increases towards the middle of the book, so that we have two lines in a canto instead of one. In cantos vi, vii, and viii Spenser has to shift the line within the canto. In each instance he has to provide a bridge. In stanza 16 of canto vi Serena and Timias see the tableau of Mirabella, as yet unnamed and identified only as a "fair maiden" on a "mangy iade" led by a "lewd foole." The next stanza assures the reader of a full explanation later:

> But by what meanes that shame to her befell . . .
> I must a while forbeare to you to tell,

because he must now pick up the Arthur line:

> Till that, as comes by course, I doe recite
> What fortune to the Briton Prince did lite.

The two other shifts of line are similarly handled, by direct statement that Spenser is dropping one line and picking up another:

> But turne we now backe to that Ladie free
> Whom we left ryding vpon an Asse. (vii, 27)

The change of line in canto viii, like that in vi, incorporates a promise to return and tell "the great aduenture" that divided Arthur from his companions, Timias and Sir Enias. This promise Spenser did not live to keep.

In both the narrative summaries and the narrative bridges Spenser is less the obtrusive author than the eighteenth and nineteenth century novelists who follow his practice. For one thing he does not use these passages for thematic commentary, only for narrative convenience. His apparatus for thematic commentary is quite distinct. For another thing, Spenser is far closer to the tradition of oral recitation of narrative by a professional entertainer, courtly minstrel or wandering bard, than was, for instance Thackeray. The passages in *Vanity Fair* in which Thackeray assumes the role of puppet master are artificial when compared with Spenser's statement that he must return to the unplowed furrow. The "I" of this passage is Spenser in his character of courtly entertainer and reflects a state of things not very far in the past when the *Faerie Queene* was published. In fact, there is nothing intrinsically impossible in the notion that the first "publication" of the *Faerie Queene* was an author's reading before an audience.

These extrinsic forecasts and bridges, delivered either omnisciently or from the assumed character of the reciter, have their intrinsic counterparts in plants, which serve the same purpose of preparing the reader for a subsequent development, but are an integral part of the narrative line, episode, or incident. Spenser makes little use of the plant, possibly because the romance convention deriving from earlier oral recital sanctions the extrinsic forecast. Spenser's preferred place for the introduction of exposition is when it is needed, rather than earlier. However, Book VI contains one good sample of a plant. Melibee, we read, was

> by common voice esteemed
> The father of the fayrest *Pastorell*,
> And of her selfe in very deede so deemed. (ix, 14)

And then we get the information that Melibee had found Pastorella in the open fields and brought her up as his own child. This, of course, prepares for the recognition scene in canto xii. I have found no other clear sample of a plant in Book VI, and this is perhaps not wholly intrinsic; at least it requires an omniscient author, even though he does not impart the information in direct address.

More intrinsic is the designing of narrative lines so that after having diverged they can converge. The Arthur-Timias line illustrates this pattern. After diverging when Arthur leaves Timias and Serena with the Hermit (v, 41) they converge when Arthur and Enias find Timias captive to Disdain and Scorn (viii, 4). So with Serena-Calepine and Calidore-

Pastorella. But there is, of course, no final and permanent convergence, in the manner of a Shakespearean comedy, for we never reach act five of the *Faerie Queene*.

A more important intrinsic unifying pattern is that of repetition and parallel, with contrast or variation. In some of the books of the *Faerie Queene*, the use of contrasting parallels functioning on both thematic and narrative levels is architectural. Such are the House of Pride and the House of Holiness in Book I, the Castle of Alma and Acrasia's Bower in Book II, the characters of Una and Duessa in Book I, Amoret and Belphebe in Book III. Book VI is less schematically constucted, its symmetry is flowing rather than static, and so the parallels are less visible, in fact can be mistaken for unskillful repetitions: the lovemaking of Priscilla and Aladine in that of Serena and Calepine; the vita of the Hermit, who was once a famous knight, in that of Melibee, who left a life at court; the rescue of Serena in that of Pastorella; Calidore's delivery of Pastorella from the tiger in the immediately following delivery from the Brigands.

A closer inspection, however, shows that little more than a motif is repeated. In each case the motif is sketchy in the first appearance, in the second magnified and varied into a new incident. Priscilla and Aladine are making love when the Knight of the Barge breaks in on them; so are Calepine and Serena when Calidore interrupts. But the Knight of the Barge's intervention is intentional and violent, Calidore's accidental and immediately covered by an apology. Aladine's injuries are outward, Serena's inward. Injury to Priscilla's reputation is avoided by the courtesy of Calidore, but ironically, he cannot prevent or cure Serena's wound, for which he is unintentionally responsible. Spenser seems to be showing how many variations he can make on the same motif.

So with the Hermit and Melibee. Both have retired from fame to simplicity. The Hermit draws from his experience the treatment which heals Timias and Serena. Once he does that, his function is served and the story moves away from him. Melibee's disillusioning experiences at court are the basis of his praise of the pastoral life. Perhaps there is a parallel between the Hermit's cure and Melibee's providing something which Spenser apparently thought Calidore lacked, a love. But, as with the Priscilla-Aladine and Calepine-Serena parallel, there is irony: Melibee's pastoral simplicity is soon smashed by the inrushing Brigands. And like Calepine-Serena, Melibee's part is not soon terminated—he remains in the story until his death in the raid of Brigands.

The same relationship is even clearer in the two rescues. Besides being briefer and simpler than Calidore's rescue of Pastorella, Calepine's rescue of Serena is thematically different. The Cannibals are only ignorant and superstitious folk, whose unnatural actions permit some extenuation. They capture Serena only for food. Then their priest persuades them to give up their claim in favor of their god's, and they accede to Serena's sacrifice. Not very far from natural men, they have deviated only a little way from natural goodness, when compared with the Brigands. These are perversions of civilized man, who have deserted lawful labor for pillage. They do not eat or sacrifice their captives; they sell them into slavery. Where the Cannibals are restrained by their priest, the Brigands have no religion and no priest. Their own lust and cupidity defeat them. Calidore effects his rescue only after the bloody quarrel between the chief and the other Brigands has weakened their strength.

This pattern of simple preliminary statement of a motif and more complicated development may also explain the awkwardly placed incident of Calidore's delivery of Pastorella from the tiger. It immediately precedes the incursion of the Brigands, and so may be intended as preparation for the more difficult rescue. To speculate on Spenser's intention is not, however, to justify the incident

Mode

THE STAPLE NARRATIVE of the *Faerie Queene* is of the romance mode. The characteristics of the romance mode of narrative are well known and have been accurately described. However, "romance" does not describe the whole narrative of the work. Spenser uses a number of other modes, which have been commonly lumped together as "allegory" but which in fact differ from one another in many ways. Of Book VI of the *Faerie Queene* these statements are true, but with a difference. Spenser was no common workman putting together a structure from prefabricated parts. Theme controls the nature of the narrative and the kinds of narrative in Book VI as it does in all parts of the work.

When we come to make a systematic analysis of the narrative modes of the book, we find that the romance mode is somewhat different from what it is in other books, and that the other modes are less employed and are also adapted to the theme. In fact, the romance narrative of Book VI is at the lower limit of what we can legitimately call romance. Some might even prefer to put it at the upper limit of what Frye calls the "high mimetic." A repetition of some of the stigmata of romance will demonstrate the marginal nature of the romance of Book VI: "a world in which the ordinary laws of nature are slightly suspended . . . prodigies of courage and endurance . . . enchanted weapons, talking animals, terrifying ogres and witches, and talismans of miraculous power."

Most of these elements are lacking in Book VI, though abundant elsewhere in the *Faerie Queene*. Of magic, either benign or malign, one finds little. The Salvage Man's invulnerability is one instance, the disappearance of the dancing maidens perhaps another. The Briana-Crudor and the Matilde-Sir Bruin episodes have some suggestions of magic. The practice of cutting off knight's beards and ladies's tresses must have been magical in origin, as in the story of Samson in Judges. Likewise, the story of the childless Matilde and Sir Bruin who receive as an heir the baby Calepine rescues from a bear has totemistic suggestions, and there is also a prophecy.* These are both far-off reminiscences rather than full-blown magic.

For the rest, there are no magical weapons, or enchantments, or witches, or the like. Calidore has a sword, but it is not magic; it is not even named, like Artegall's Chrysaor. Arthur has apparently stored the shield which blinds his enemies; at least he isn't using it in Book VI. There are none of the mythic occurrences like the soul shifting brothers

---

* A more immediate meaning appears below, p. 71.

Priamond, Diamond, and Triamond in Book IV; no nature deities like Proteus or Cymoent, no metamorphoses or enchanted springs.

Even more remarkable is the absence of the malign magical. Every other book has one or more evil magicians, male or female, Archimago, Duessa, Acrasia, Busirane, the six-handed Gereoneo. In every book but the sixth we encounter one or more embodiments of evil energy, whose origins lie far back in racial history, in black magic, in the demonic subconscious forces that are masked by the veneer of civilization but sometimes break from under the surface to terrify us. Many of these are Spenser's finest creations. To anyone possessed of more than a superficial understanding of human behavior a character like Pyrochles with his compulsion towards self-destruction strikes home. We do not find his like in Book VI. As a result the book lacks the ability to evoke the blood-chilling terror of other books.

This is no defect. In fact, it is a measure of Spenser's artistic control that he so successfully avoids the demonic and the magical. Courtesy, as Spenser conceives it, applies neither to the heights nor to the depths of human experience, but to the surface. In the proem to the book he tells us that the blossom of "comely courtesy,"

> Which though it on a lowly stalke doe bowre,
> Yet brancheth forth in braue nobilitie,
> And spreds it selfe through all ciuilitie.

That is where courtesy flowers, in civility, in the daily affairs of ordinary men living with one another. Magic, however, is an expression of other levels of human experience, both below and above. Benign magic is super-natural aid to counter the malign magic that thrusts up from the pit. Neither therefore has any place in a book devoted to courtesy. If you want dragons slain, send for Redcross, not Calidore.

Other elements of romance are quite appropriate to courtesy. In fact, in design and movement Book VI is the most romance-like of all the books of the *Faerie Queene*. The substance is almost totally narrative, and the narrative is all of action. Aside from a few complaints and Melibee's praise of simple life, one finds only occasional stanzas of philosophical commentary.

Romances happen in fairyland, which is originally the Celtic other-world, one of whose striking characteristics is the suspension of time. It is not that time is faster or slower; it can be either. A mortal can discover that what he thought was a few years spent in the other world was actually a century. Alternatively, he can enter the other world, spend days or months, and return to find his companions still eating the same meal they were when he left.

The origin of this fluidity of time is not so important as what Spenser does with it. He found it a magnificent tool for his purposes. First, it enables him to treat reality at a remove, something most critics since Wordsworth have found desirable, if art is not to be mere documentation. Second, in a fluid time, reality can be abstracted from actuality more easily, for events can be abstracted from time. Sans time, events can have a pattern, Aristotle's beginning, middle and end, which they cannot in time, which has no beginning, middle, or end.

This freeing of events from time renders credible two features of romance retained in Book VI, the "Prodigies of courage and endurance," listed by Frye and the use of coincidence, which he does not mention because, though characteristic, it is not specific to romance.

The heroes of Book VI are certainly not ordinary folk. Calidore hews his way into Briana's castle with ease of a steer flicking off flies—the figure is Spenser's—and the Salvage Man slays Turpine's retainers in heaps. Calepine finds no difficulty in rescuing Serena from a band of cannibals—he merely wades into them, protected only by darkness. Calidore has to use a deception diguising himself as a shepherd, to gain access to Pastorella, but he knocks out the Brigands about as easily as Calepine does the Cannibals. But so far as we are told all is achieved by natural means, no cloaks of invisibility of invincibility, no shields that blind the enemy.

The means whereby Calidore and Calepine are so puissant may escape the casual reader. In Book II Spenser makes it quite clear that Arthur, deprived of his own sword and his spear broken, holds off and finally kills both Cymocles and Pyrochles, by the superiority of his tactics:

> And suffered rash Pyrochles waste his idel might.

Arthur may not be stronger, more courageous, or even better trained, but he is in full possession of his wits, not driven by passion like Pyrochles. In other words, moral superiority results in better tactics, which produce victory. I believe we are to understand that Calidore fights his way into Briana's castle by the same moral-tactical superiority. The Cannibals are barbarians, superstitious and gross, and the Brigands are lawless and corrupt, hence weak. Calepine and Calidore can vanquish numbers of them. You can see the same principle at work in any television horse opera. Apparently the Salvage Man is an exception. However, Spenser has made a point of the fact that, despite his present appearance, he is of good lineage. Turpine and his retainers, though apparently of better condition, are probably base born and so no match for either Arthur or the Salvage Man.

A somewhat similar principle will render coincidence credible. Surely it plays a large part in Book VI. Calepine, separated from Serena when he followed the bear with the baby, is in the right place at the right time to rescue her from sacrifice by the Cannibals. To be sure, he was seeking her, but we are not told that he was actually tracking her. He just happened to be there. Of all the castles to which Calidore might have taken Pastorella, he chose the one occupied by her lost parents.

These are not quite the desperate expedient of a harried script writer pressed for time and dry in invention. Behind them lies a thematic narrative justification, just as with the prowess of Calidore. When events are abstracted from time, and so from actuality, they can be patterned, and this pattern can be an order produced by an intention. This sometimes happens in dreams, where there is a similar abstraction. It should happen in fiction designed to exemplify virtue. The proper order for Calepine and Serena is union, for they are lovers. This union has been disrupted; it must be restored by intention. That is, Calepine's search must succeed. And it does. So with Pastorella. She was born a gentlewoman, and she must again become one, which requires her being restored to her parents. Calidore has already set the reordering process to work by wooing and winning her. It is interrupted by the Brigands. After her rescue, the process or reintegration pushes one step further. She is rejoined to her parents.

In Book VI the romance mode touches the "realistic."* We notice this particularly in the use of detail and in the motivation of some of the minor personages. For the former, two illustrations will suffice. In the second episode, the depredations of the Knight of the Barge, Spenser is really performing some psychological analysis. He does this frequently in the *Faerie Queene*, but most commonly he externalizes the analysis of personality in a personification-allegory or in a mythological incident. A good sample is Scudamour's night in the Smithy of Care (IV, v, 32-45), in which the din raised by the smith and his six helpers expresses Scudamour's doubts and jealousy. In Book VI the same sort of analysis is done in representional detail. The Knight of the Barge projects his own insecurity on his lady, first abandoning her to take Priscilla away from Aladine and then, when Priscilla flees, taking out his frustration by making his lady walk, while he on horse prods her with his spear. Spenser presents this quite objectively, with no interpretation.

Another illustration of representational detail comes when Calidore accidentally interrupts the lovemaking of Calepine and Serena. He instantly

* I do not like the word "realistic" in this sense, because it begs the question. It is doubtful if any author ever tried to communicate unreality. The differentiation is rather in modes of reality and methods of communication. What most critics mean when they write "realistic" is that the method of communicating the reality is by the representation of externals. An artist who represents the reality of a horse, as he apprehends it, by drawing a recognizable image of a horse is a "realist," the more attention he pays to external details the more "realistic." Another artist can communicate the reality he apprehends by a series of waving and curling lines. We generally call him an abstractionist. I shall call the first artist "representational."

apologizes. The modest Serena, however, is too embarrassed to remain. She wanders off, covering her embarrassment by picking flowers. It is at this moment that the Blattant Beast rushes out of the forest and bites her—a juxtaposition of the representational and the symbolic. What Spencer is saying is that the victims of Slander are not the brazen creatures who flaunt their disrespect for convention, but the innocents, caught in easily misunderstood situations, whose innate reticence gives Slander its opportunity. I believe I detect a further refinement. Serena may not be so much embarrassed by her own plight as by Calidore's. She is embarrassed at his embarrassment.

We have noted the absence of malign magic in the villainous characters. In fact, there are no villains in Book VI, not even the Blattant Beast. There are only opposite characters, not real antagonists. An antagonist or a villain has to be somewhere near the protagonist in power and station. The opposite characters of Book VI are all inferior to the principals not only in virtue but also in capability. Even the Blattant Beast is not really monstrous. He bites only the weak and defenseless; against Calidore his only recourse is flight and when Calidore finally bays him he becomes a whimpering dog. Briana, Crudor, Turpine, the Cannibals, the Brigands are just selfish and mean individuals who thoughtlessly invade the dignity of others. Their main defect is lack of sensitivity, even intelligence. You cannot hate them; rather you laugh at them. The Cannibals and the Brigands have to be suppressed, of course. The others only have to be retrained. Turpine is baffled—surely someone came by and cut him down before he suffered more than severe humiliation—and Calidore pities Briana and Crudor enough to set straight their affairs.

This analysis of the narrative of Book VI as marginally romance with elements of both high and low mimetic modes fits the bulk of the book. It also establishes another point about Spenser's narrative technique: neither as a whole nor in specific blocks does it fit any category. Of all authors Spenser is least useful as a provider of neat illustrations of form and mode. There are overlappings and underlyings that baffle attempts at simplicity. When we view a certain episode we may call it romance, but at the same time confess it has other characteristics. For instance, the episode of Briana and Crudor is accurately called an exemplum, a story told to make a homiletic point. You could also call it a parable. It defines discourtesy (in Briana and Crudor) and courtesy (in Calidore) just as the parable of the Good Samaritan defines "neighbor." But perhaps "exemplum" and "parable" are more thematic entities than narrative.

That is not so true of a group of modes usually lumped together as "allegorical." Here the nature of the narrative grows out of the theme, to be sure, but the difference extends from purpose to method. For instance, in the episodes that have a mythological basis, the structure of the narrative differs from that in the romance episodes. In genesis, mythology is not allegorical, but it had become so to sophisticated intellectuals hundreds of years before Spenser and it is so in Spenser's time, as can be seen in such mythographical manuals as Natale Conti's.

To Spenser mythology is sometimes a method of externalizing for narrative use certain conceptualized psychic forces which singly or in combination create personality. The best demonstration of this method is the sixth canto of Book III, which is really an exposition of the differences in personality between Amoret and Belphebe, two apparently opposite types of womanhood, passive and active, yielding and aggressive. Amoret is characteristically in someone's power. She is freed from Busirane only to be kidnaped by Lust. Belphebe characteristically tortures Timias with her coldness or jealousy. The understanding of the narrative depends on this differentiation, whereas the understanding of the theme requires that we see the two women as manifestations of the same femininity. Into the making of the episode (it is not a digression) go such bits of classical mythology as the stories of Danae and Leda and of Venus and Diana, the whole fitted into a philosophical frame.

Book VI contains nothing so comprehensive, but the description of the Blattant Beast, particularly the genealogies, is of the same sort. The first genealogy, given by Calidore to Artegall in explanation of his quest, is that the Blattant Beast was begotten by Cerberus on Chimera and grew up in "Stygian fen."* The other, given by the Hermit who undertakes the healing of Timias and Serena, gives the Beast Typhaon and Echidna as parents. The disparity is more apparent than real. All the parents are products of misalliances; Spenser is using them as symbols of disorder.

The Blattant Beast is, however, not entirely mythological. It is also a personification of Slander. Envy and Detraction call it into the story to attack Artegall, and Despetto, Defetto, and Decetto set it on Timias. The effects of its bite and the manner of its entrances into the story both show that it is partly conceived as a personification, in the manner of the *Romance of the Rose* or of a morality play. One of the marks of personification-allegory is the absence of self-standing action. The actions of a personification only externalize its conceptual reality. Slander never does anything but slander, and it needs no reason for slandering beyond its own essence.

Spenser sometimes uses personification in this pure form. Envy and Detraction in Book V, xii, are examples. More often, however, he veils the personification, by using foreign words or by distorting words. Des-

---

* One indication that the creative process is the same for the Blattant Beast as for the Garden of Adonis is the use of the phrase "to perfect ripness grew" in both accounts to denote the maturation of the Blattant Beast and of Amoret (III, vii, 52 and VI, i, 8).

petto, Defetto, and Decetto are Despite, Defect, and Deceit in Italianate guise.

Analogy, the rhetorical figures of metaphor or simile, can also be the basis of narrative. The episode of the healing of Timias and Serena is built on an analogy between the social effects of slander and the physical effects of a bite which inflicts an infected wound. Once he sets up the analogy, however, Spenser quickly abandons it in favor of more literal statement. The Hermit applies no salves, performs no surgery, but rather gives counsel to minds: subdue desire, use scant diet, shun secrecy. Spenser seems to be wavering between the conception of the hermit as a physician and as a confessor. The analogy of physician and confessor is a commonplace in pastoral and devotional literature of the later middle ages, particularly that of the friars, and Spenser's readers no doubt inherited it. Possibly they found no difficulty in what seems to us a sudden switch from metaphor to literal statement. The modern reader may think of the Hermit as a psychiatrist treating a psychosomatic illness, but this is a desperate expedient. More likely, Spenser's imagination was for the moment less than normally resourceful and, anyway, he is in a hurry to get Timias and Serena back in the story.

Personification and analogy join in the episode of Mirabella, which begins immediately after the cure of Timias and Serena, but is sidetracked for Arthur's punishment of Turpine. Disdain and Scorn, Mirabella's persecutors, are obviously pure personifications, Mirabella herself probably a veiled one, but the narrative development is rather different from that in the Timias-Belphebe story. The episode of Mirabella begins like a tableau or an emblem, a static picture composed of visualized symbolic elements: mangy horse, downcast lady, the fool Scorn whipping her, the churl Disdain leading her horse.

Then Spenser provides an explanation for the tableau, like a museum guide commenting at length on a painting. Mirabella is a haughty lady whose cruelty to her suitors brought her into the disfavor of Cupid, who hailed her into court, tried her, and assigned a penance.* Up to this point the episode is static, a tableau with elaborate commentary, but it now becomes a story, somewhat as the opening still shot of a movie may break into motion. Timias rushes into the scene to save Mirabella, is beaten by Disdain, and has to be rescued by Arthur.

One other variety of narrative usually labelled "allegorical" finds only slight illustration in Book VI, that incorporating by allusion historical events and personages and variously called "historical," "political," or

---

* The elaborate legal imagery suggests an ecclesiastical rather than a civil court. Ecclesiastical courts had tried sexual offenses and had frequently assigned penances, such as marching around the church every Sunday for a period of time wearing sackcloth and carrying a candle.

"topical" allegory, or "roman à clef." The attempt to identify characters and incidents in the *Faerie Queene* with actual personages and happenings and then to find in these identifications the meaning of an episode has been a blind alley for Spenserian scholarship. The endeavor would not be worth mention here if the first appearance of the Blattant Beast in Book V, xii did not occur immediately after incidents obviously intended as topical allusions. The names of the characters, Irena, Belga, Borbon, Flordelis, point unmistakably to Spenser's intention to reflect in his narrative certain events of the recent past in Ireland, the Low Countries, and France.

If Borbon is unmistakably Henry IV of France and his suit to Flordelis Henry's claim to the throne, the disagreement among scholars as to the identity of Artegall, who restores Flordelis to Borbon, is a clue to Spenser's thematic and narrative method. He is not primarily commenting on or interpreting history; he is constructing a narrative to exemplify his theme, the achievement of justice in foreign affairs. To understand either narrative or theme it is not necessary for us to know whether Artegall is Arthur Lord Grey, Sir John Norris, or the Earl of Essex, or, as is more probable, sometimes one, sometimes another. Doubtless, to Spenser's readers, or that portion of them knowledgeable in foreign affairs, the episode of the Blattant Beast's attack on Artegall had an extra sharpness of effect, the joy of recognition. But Spenser is writing fiction, not history. He can find materials in current or past events, just as he can find them in myth, legend, literary sources, or where not.

Josephine Waters Bennett, who has worked out the topical references in the last two cantos of Book V, provides us with some clues to the actual creative process. Some of the allusions are pertinent only after 1594, and this added to some bibliographical evidence makes it likely that the incident of the Blattant Beast in Book V was written after the composition of Book VI and added during or soon before the actual printing. If this line of evidence is valid, then Spenser's procedure was somewhat like this: he first created the Blattant Beast from mythological and personification material, including only very generalized topical or historical allusions. These are in Calidore's pursuit of the Beast from court to city, to town, to country in canto ix, and the account of the Beast's ravages among the clergy in canto xii. It is in a monastery church that Calidore finally bays the animal. Then, as a happy afterthought, he added the Beast's attack on Artegall as a prelude to Book VI, much as Pope added the celestial machinery of the *Rape of the Lock* in the second edition. Hence, the topical allusion to the slander and detraction that met Sir John Norris after his return from Ireland is merely illustrative, not essential.

Both topical allusion and mythology appear in the episode on Mount

Acidale in which Calidore sees the naked maidens dancing to Colin Clout's piping. The episode is only thematically connected with the preceding and following incidents, the pastoral life of Arcady and the killing of the tiger that attacks Pastorella. The thematic connection would be a bit clearer, if the incident of the tiger had preceded and the raid of the Brigands immediately followed, for the episode of Mount Acidale seems to be a thematic preparation for the raid of the Brigands. It is not enclosed in the usual sense of explaining or motivating the incident that encloses it; in fact it is not expository and so must serve another function.

Calidore's sight of the hundred dancing maidens circling round the Graces who in turn circle round Rosalind is an epiphany. Many of the traditional features of the epiphany are discernible: Calidore is atop a mountain, he sees things denied to mundane vision, namely the Graces, who are divine; Colin Clout functions partly as his guide, though only after the disappearance of the dancing maidens. The differences between this and the more easily recognized epiphany in which Redcross, guided by Heavenly Contemplation, beholds the New Jerusalem (I, x, 46-57) are dictated by the same thematic considerations that remove magic from the romance narrative of Book VI.*

Both epiphanies, interestingly, incorporate topical or historical allusions. Redcross learns his ancestry of Saxon kings and is identified with St. George; Colin Clout brings the scene into topical focus by directly addressing Gloriana-Elizabeth, praying pardon for making Rosalind the center of the dancers. One could point further parallels: both epiphanies come at about the same point in the book, canto x; both serve as preludes to the appearance of evil, the old Dragon and the raid of the Brigands; and both seem to be preparations for the eventual success of the quest, though the latter parallel is not exact.

The relationship of the epiphany on Mount Acidale to the incidents that precede and follow it is a clue to understanding the combination of narrative modes we find in Book VI. Mythology, personification-allegory, topical allusion, epiphany all appear in small amounts in a narrative that is dominantly romance. The quantity of these other modes is singly or in sum hardly more than enough to flavor the whole, like raisins and nuts in a pudding. They produce variety in texture.

They could be disturbing elements, if not blended properly. Possibly some readers find the epiphany on Mount Acidale or the tableau of Mirabella so. What does Spenser mean by mixing such elements? If he wants a narrative mode locked into actuality, as representational realism is, why does he destroy the tone by incorporating other modes at a far greater

* The thematic meaning of this epiphany is developed below, p. 57.

remove from actuality? Isn't he really dangerously near sliding into bathos?

No, Spenser's practice permits him the best of several worlds. For thematic reasons, he wished to put courtesy into the everyday world, but he does not deny that there are other worlds above, below, and around the everyday world. These other worlds are closer or farther; their denizens sometimes invade the everyday world. So the fictional world he creates is open on all sides. A little journey takes you cross the border, which is not very fixed anyway. The balance of representational detail and timeless romance puts Spenser in a strategic position to move, but not too far, in any direction. Magic is a bit too far, so he does not let magic invade his world. Mount Acidale is only a convenient walk from the Arcady, which is only several days' ride from Briana's castle. Too, Mount Acidale is not very steep; you never get above the clouds, as you do when you ascend the Mount of Contemplation near the House of Holiness.

The thematic purpose is not the only reason why Spenser did not choose to abandon completely these other modes, though he might mute them. The incomplete narrative lines of Book VI, Arthur, Timias, Calepine-Serena, the Salvage Man show that Spenser was planning further books of the *Faerie Queene*. A section of one of them remains, the Mutability Cantos, to show that Spenser intended to use the mythological on an even bigger scale than in the Garden of Adonis. The Mutability Cantos of Book VII would not have come as a shock to the reader while the Mount Acidale episode of Book VI persisted in his mind. We can speculate that Spenser had not permanently abandoned magic, black or white, or personification-allegory either.

II

THEME

Thematic Line

THE EFFORT TO SEPARATE narrative from theme, means from purpose, is always dangerous, more in major writers than in minor, certainly nowhere more than with the *Faerie Queene*. Here thematic interpretation has been so attractive as to lead all but a few critics into almost complete neglect of narrative structure. This I hope I have avoided by beginning with narrative. In passing next to theme I cannot hope to avoid repetition, for I intend to follow thematic lines, incident by incident, as I have the narrative lines. The order of the incidents will be somewhat rearranged so as to follow thematic developments interrupted and dovetailed in the narrative. Thus Calepine and Serena will be followed straight through their adventures, rather than as presented. I cannot, however, do that with Calidore, whose activities frame the book, enclosing the other thematic lines.

The subject of Book VI is courtesy. It would be conventional, but false to Spenser's method, to begin with a comprehensive definition. If we proceed with Spenser we begin only with the general notion that courtesy is grown in the sacred nursery of virtue from heavenly seed. Though the nursery affords no fairer flower, it grows on a lowly stalk and spreads through all civility. It is easily overlooked or misappreciated. This, plus the etymology of courtesy from court, is what Spenser tells us in the proem, and it is enough to start with.

In this figurative working definition there are three principal elements: courtesy is a virtue; it is lowly, that is, it functions on a lower level of human endeavor than some other virtues, holiness, for example, or even justice; its proper locus is "civility," that is, it deals with the relationships between private individuals in society, rather than between organized groups, such as states, or between man and the supernatural. These are the limits within which Spenser proposes to treat the virtue of courtesy.

The book dealing with courtesy will, then, be an exploration of the uses and abuses of courtesy, told in narrative, various incidents of which will illustrate and exemplify courtesy in specific situations. We will see it practiced, unpracticed, and malpracticed. If narrative and theme are perfectly fused, every incident, every character, every detail will have some bearing on courtesy. That bearing need not be direct and obvious, so that every action will be a direct, conscious expression of some character's courtesy or discourtesy. Some leeway must be left for accident and fortune. But there should be some bearing, direct or indirect.

41

The presentation of courtesy begins with a sketch of discourtesy. The Blattant Beast, whose suppression Calidore, the champion of courtesy, undertakes, appears first in Book V. Artegall, returning from his successful quest, is reviled by the hags Envy and Detraction, who set the Beast on him. The Beast does nothing more than bark and the hags no more than scold. Artegall will not allow Talus to silence Detraction, leaving it to Calidore, who has the mission of muzzling it. That the champion of justice leaves the Blattant Beast to the champion of courtesy clearly means that courtesy and discourtesy lie beyond the scope, or at least the power, of justice, which, formalized as law, can deal with many evils, but not effectively with the one personified by the Blattant Beast.

Narrowly understood, the Blattant Beast is slander, detraction, backbiting, libel—all those irresponsible attacks by mouth or pen on the integrity of individual character. The powerlessness of law to deal with slander needs no elaboration. But why is slander singled out among the many kinds of discourtesy as the vice to be personified as the antagonist in the book of courtesy? Surely slander is only one kind of discourtesy. True, and we meet many other kinds. But they have all one essential element, a selfishness, a blindness to the sensibilities and needs of others. This is the essence of slander. Just as the sin of Adam, though specifically disobedience, contained within it, as theologians always argued, every other kind of sin, so slander contains within it every kind of discourtesy. More importantly, the only remedy for slander is active courtesy.

That Envy and Detraction call the Blattant Beast into the story means that slander, and indeed all discourtesy, arise from the need of some to make themselves equal by pulling down what is superior. Courtesy, as we shall see, has much to do with the recognition of one's proper place in the social order, and recognizing that both one's superior and one's inferior each has his rights in his proper place.

Spenser provides two clues to the understanding of the nature of the Blattant Beast. One is etymological. The word "blattant," coined by Spenser seems to derive from Βλάπτω, hurt, hinder, lame, impede.* It is of the nature of all forms of discourtesy that they hurt someone. The discourteous person seems to find no way of helping himself except by hurting someone else. The official psychology and ethics of Spenser's time had not yet made the discovery that most people who hate others also hate themselves, but Spenser seems often to know this fact intuitively. Many of Spenser's discourteous people seem at war with themselves, disordered within. The courteous person helps himself by helping others.

The other clue is the mythological parentage of the Beast. He is the offspring of Cerberus and Chimera in one account (i, 8) and of Echidna

---

* See below, p. 67, for amplification of the meaning "blattant."

and Typhon in the other (vi, 9-11). The contradiction is only apparent, since Cerberus and Chimera are children of Echidna and Typhon, and all are monsters, expressions of disorder. The physical properties of the Beast carry out this notion of monstrosity. Never particularly described, the Beast seems part dog—Cerberus perhaps—and part wild boar. Its nature combines timidity and fierceness. Calidore cannot bay it, but the moment Serena wanders away from the protection of Calepine and Calidore it dashes out of the bush to carry her off. Every discourteous person we meet in the story shares these characteristics, boldness and violence in the face of their inferiors, cowardice towards their equals.

The Beast's adversary is Calidore. His name, of course, means "beautiful gift," and Spenser early tells us (ii, 2) that perfect courtesy, such as Calidore exemplifies, must be a gift of nature. Peculiar to the gently born, it is not universal even to that class. It cannot be acquired in its perfection, though the painful effort to be courteous in those not naturally endowed is praiseworthy. Courtesy is sometimes lacking in those of great intellectual power. This analysis is perfectly realized in Calidore. Without apparent thought or effort, he is able to put himself into the place of everyone he meets, whether high or low. He never acts rashly or thoughtlessly, but always seems to perceive the true meaning of the actions of others. He treats inferiors as he would wish to be treated were he an inferior.

After a brief introduction of Calidore, "whose gracious speach did steale mens hearts away," so that although "well approu'd" in arms he was best loved for his "faire vsage and conditions sound," the action commences with the meeting of Calidore and Artegall, the incoming and the outgoing champions. Artegall has seen the Blattant Beast, and recites his recent experiences. This meeting has the thematic significance that discourtesy is beyond the scope of justice, and so Calidore must complete the work of Artegall.

The first episode of Briana and Crudor makes this point clear. Calidore has scarcely left Artegall when he comes on a squire tied to a tree. From the squire he learns that the lady of the neighboring castle, Briana, has her servants waylay travelers and cut the hair of the ladies and the beards of the knights. With the hair Briana weaves a mantle for her love, Crudor, with which she hopes to win him. Doubtless, this is illegal and a sufficiently large police force could stop such proceedings. Usually however, police forces are too busy with thefts and murders to afford much protection against such minor offenses as harassing telephone calls and littering one's property with empty beer bottles. The sort of practice Briana is engaged in falls into the same category. The loss of the victims is not great in terms that a court could assess. How much value can be put on a beard in a suit for damages? Yet it is a real evil, for it is an invasion of the personal dignity of the victim. The knight's beard is the symbol of his virility, and the lady's hair of her modesty. It was in Spenser's day and still is a common practice to disgrace public women by cutting off their hair.

The method of handling the evil by Calidore is also an illustration of the difference between justice and courtesy. Calidore has to use force, the instrument of law, to force his way into the castle, has in fact to kill the seneschal who carries out Briana's orders. But once inside, Calidore endures Briana's insults, refusing to reply in kind, and abides the arrival of Crudor when she sends for him. Calidore's solution of the evil depends on Crudor. Again, Calidore has to fight, but only for the purpose of making the two listen to reason. When Crudor is overcome, Calidore does not kill him, nor does he bind Briana.

Instead, he penetrates to the cause of the evil custom. Briana is only reacting to the low estimation in which Crudor holds her. He will not love her for herself, but demands a price, the mantle. The obvious solution is to make him see how selfish his attitude is and to accept Briana's love forthwith. This is a real solution, because the cause of the evil is now eliminated. And Calidore manages the affair so that the two become his friends. He spends some time with them amiably while he is recovering from his wounds.

The next episode continues the exemplification of courtesy. Calidore sees a young lad dressed in huntsman's garb kill a knight. This is a violation of due order, of which courtesy is a part: knights fight knights and commoners fight commoners. However, Calidore does not charge Tristram, the young huntsman, and beat him down. This, too would have been a violation of order. Instead, Calidore demands the reason: "Why hath thy hand too bold it selfe embrewed / In blood of knight, the which by thee is slaine / By thee, no knight; which armes impugneth plaine?" Calidore is right; someone has violated the social order, but it was the slain knight, not Tristram.

The Knight of the Barge is a classic study in the irresponsible use of force for selfish ends. He has come on Aladine and Priscilla wooing—innocently Spenser assures us—and has taken advantage of Aladine's being unarmed to beat him and to try to seize Priscilla, despite the fact that he has a lady companion of his own. By one act he has managed to hurt three people. When Priscilla flees, the Knight of the Barge takes out his frustration on his own lady, making her walk while he on horseback prods her with his lance. When Tristram protests, he again takes advantage of his superiority in both rank and arms to charge Tristram, who is on foot and armed only with a slender dart. The Knight of the Barge is undoubtedly a pathological personality, whose modern equivalent raids parked cars in lovers' lanes. One wonders whether, had Calidore arrived a few minutes earlier, he would have been able to rehabilitate this distorted creature as he did Crudor and Briana.

Since the Knight of the Barge is dead, Calidore's task is to pick up the pieces. First, his lady is given Tristram for an escort. Then Calidore finds Priscilla lamenting over the wounded Aladine. Priscilla is close to hysteria: she cannot think of any way to get Aladine to safety. Subconsciously, as we later discover, she is concerned for her own compromised situation. She is away from home against her parents' will, in the company of a man they have forbidden her to see, and their tryst threatens to become a matter of public record. There is also a third element. Priscilla is a courteous person, which means that, even in her plight, she habitually thinks about other people. Hence, she hesitates to ask Calidore to help. He is a stranger, and besides that a knight, whose dignity would be impaired by physical labor.

Calidore is equal to the demands of Priscilla's situation. First, he sheds all false dignity. He puts Aladine on his shield and he and Priscilla carry him home. With Aladine safe in the care of his father, Calidore can turn to Priscilla's care. She is naturally concerned about the scandal which may ensue, and so, when he revives, is Aladine. They have to trust Calidore, who proves not merely sympathetic but resourceful. Since Priscilla has spent the night away from home, Calidore must cover for her. He cannot say that she spent it with Aladine's family, for the whole reason why Aladine and Priscilla met as they did is that her parents are trying to marry her to a powerful neighboring lord.

Calidore solves the difficulty by first returning to the slain Knight of the Barge, cutting off his head, and carrying it with him as proof of the story he will tell her parents. Courtesy, as practiced by Calidore, requires the truth, but not necessarily the whole truth. He actually tells Priscilla's parents that he rescued her from a discourteous knight who tried to abduct her, and since he has the head, they accept his oath on his knighthood that she is "most perfect pure, and guiltless innocent."

Some interesting generalizations about slander particularly and discourtesy generally emerge from the story of Priscilla and Aladine. For one, the possibility of sheer mischance. The young couple are in no way to blame for what happened. They can hardly be indicted even of indiscretion, for they had no other way of seeing each other except in secret. Spenser does not specifically blame the parents of Priscilla, but the implication is strong. The concern of Aladine for Priscilla's reputation is also illustrative of the nature of courtesy.

The outcome of the Priscilla-Aladine episode is, thanks to Calidore's understanding and skill, fortunate. The next episode, that of Serena and Calepine, is not so quickly concluded. Spenser tells the Priscilla-Aladine story in straightforward, literal terms. Hence, having established a pattern, he can use the quicker and more suggestive method of symbol for the next story. The initial situation is identical, a young couple innocently making love in a secret tryst.

45

It is no psychopath who interrupts their wooing, but Calidore himself. He instantly apologizes for his intrusion, and Calepine, after initial annoyance, accepts the apology in proper spirit, asking Calidore to sit down and visit a while. But the damage has been done. Serena wanders away from the two men, ostensibly picking flowers. The Blattant Beast rushes out of the wood and seizes her. Calidore instantly gives chase, and the Beast drops Serena. But his teeth have wounded her, those iron teeth whose touch is poison.

This is not Calidore's responsibility. Calepine is unwounded and presumably able to care for Serena, while Calidore performs his primary function of pursuing the Beast.

To understand the incident, we must start with the actions and character of Serena. Why does she leave Calepine and Calidore and expose herself to the attack of the Blattant Beast? Spenser says she was allured by the mildness of the weather and the beauty of the flowers, which she began to pick. His exact words give us the clue:

> Wandred about the fields, as liking led
> Her wauering lust after her wandring sight (iii, 23).

Wander and *waver* suggest irresponsibility, *lust*, self-indulgence. I suspect also embarrassment. Innocent though their lovemaking was, apologetic as Calidore is, she does not want to face him, and so she wanders off, in other words, she follows undisciplined impulse. This seems to be her response to any unpleasant situation. When, in canto vii, Timias attacks Mirabella's tormentors and is losing, Serena flees. Of course, this is the popular romance motif of the frightened fleeing maiden, the most thorough study of which in the *Faerie Queene* is Florimell, but I believe there is more to Serena's behavior. Her flight gets her into even worse trouble than her wandering off from Calepine and Calidore. When she stops many miles later, she immediately blames Calepine for leaving her unprotected and alone. This is hardly fair, for Calepine had run into a situation that required him to take responsibility for someone else's welfare. And by the time he could discharge the responsibility, Serena was gone. Far from being alone, she was under the protection of Timias, and had chosen flight instead of staying with him.

Her capture by the Cannibals is not then entirely a misadventure. She has provided the occasion of her own peril. Indeed, before her flight, the Hermit has warned her that victims of slander must work their own cure by learning to restrain their senses. Serena has apparently not learned this lesson completely; she cannot restrain her impulse to flee the unpleasant, or to think of herself first and abandon her protector when he gets into trouble.

Her complaints against Calepine are completely unfounded. He is in fact the soul of fidelity and steadfastness. At the very moment she is complaining, he is searching everywhere for her, and it is eventually Calepine who rescues her from the Cannibals, who have stripped her and are sacrificing her to their god. Does Serena show proper gratitide? No, she is so embarrassed at being naked that she will not even speak to him, and he has to wait until morning to find her identity. Spenser makes no more of the story, promising a later continuation, which he did not live to fulfill. I cannot resist the speculation that she would have played a major role in Book VII, probably as an illustration of one kind of inconstancy.

In the encounter with Turpine Calepine's courtesy is put to the extreme test. He has sole responsibility for the wounded Serena, Calidore having ridden off in pursuit of the Blattant Beast. Serena needs Calepine's horse, since she apparently has none of her own, so that Calepine cannot use it for combat. In this situation, Calepine is faced with extreme provocation. First Turpine rides by on the other side of a river which Calepine must get Serena across. It is too deep for Calepine to wade leading the horse, and Turpine refuses any help, instead laughing at Calepine's plight. Only here does Calepine momentarily loose his self-possession. He challenges Turpine to fight him on foot. He cannot use his horse or risk the safety of Serena, should his horse be hurt in combat. Even the challenge is, though safe, unwise, for Calepine, as he later realizes, cannot hazard Serena's safety by allowing himself to be goaded into a fight.

He eventually finds passage across the river and comes to Turpine's castle. Here he endures the rudeness of the porter, and when he is told he cannot stop at the castle without fighting the lord, he declines. Instead, he elects to spend the night in the open, watching over Serena, who is "couerd with cold, and wrapt in wretchednesse." Calepine weeps, but still keeps "wary watch."

His troubles are not over. Not satisfied with denying Calepine the shelter of his castle, Turpine attacks Calepine the next morning, apparently having mistaken his forebearance for cowardice. Turpine has every advantage, since he is on horse and Calepine on foot. The account of the unequal match has one curious note: Calepine takes refuge behind Serena, who cries mercy to Turpine. Some commentators have construed this is a mark of cowardice. This seems unnecessarily hard. The exact sequence of events is not too easy to follow, the usual Spenserian mix-up of pronouns interfering with clarity.

But Calepine's taking refuge behind Serena seems only momentary. He is in a dilemma. If he stands up to Turpine he may get badly hurt or even killed, and then who will care for Serena? If he runs, who protects Serena? Hiding behind her back would seem to be an impulsive, unsuccessful attempt to resolve the contradiction. Calidore, with his superior skill, could probably have solved the problem; perhaps also Tristram, who was able to meet the Knight of the Barge on such terms. But Calepine's best is not quite good enough, he is eventually wounded, and he might have been killed but for the intervention of the Salvage Man.

The separation from Serena I would choose to regard as an unfortunate accident. Recuperated, Calepine goes out for a stroll. Once he comes on a bear with a baby in his jaws, courtesy requires a course of action. He can hardly do otherwise than attempt to rescue the baby, risking his life in an unarmed attack on the bear. When he has killed the bear, he cannot just walk away and leave the baby. If there is a conflict between his duties to Serena and to the baby, surely the baby's needs are the greater emergency. He must find the parents, and he spends hours looking for them:

> So vp and downe he wandred many a mile
> With wearie trauell and uncertain toile. (iv, 25)

He finds nobody, until evening, when he comes on the mourning Matilde. As soon as the baby is safe in her custody, Calepine refuses her invitation to come home with her and be provided with horse and arms. This would perhaps have been the wiser course, for Calepine's haste to rejoin Serena is really a delay. Calidore would doubtless have accepted the offer and the next morning, properly mounted, have caught up with Serena. But Calepine lacks Calidore's experience and maturity.

He keeps searching for Serena, who meanwhile passes from the protection of the Salvage Man into the surer one of Arthur and Timias. Calepine does not cease searching; he merely fails to find her. If we remember that Spenser's Fairyland is rough and dangerous country, unprovided with signposts and road maps, there is nothing improbable in Calepine's continued separation from Serena, certainly no dereliction on Calepine's part.

The management of the Calepine-Serena story is another proof of Spenser's grip on the essentials of the human condition. The world in which courtesy must be practiced is not dominated by reason and order. Both malice and mischance intervene to frustrate good intentions. People of good intention sometimes find themselves in situations which require more than good intentions; they require a high order of intelligence and experience. Courtesy, steadfastness, bravery are perhaps enough to avert the worst disasters—Serena is rescued from the Cannibals, but not without danger and difficulty, and not without Calepine and Serena making many mistakes and suffering from them. Virtue is intention plus skill; skill has often to be acquired the hard way.

The Salvage Man who rescues Serena and Calepine from Turpine, and the Cannibals who capture Serena have something in common. Both are outside the limits of civilization. The words *salvage* and *cannibal* can seriously mislead the uninitiated. "Salvage" as the text always spells it, has no connotation of ferocity or cruelty, though the Salvage Man is on occasion ferocious enough, but never cruel. The word merely means that he dwells in the woods and partakes somewhat of the nature of the woods and its denizens. It is tempting to view him as a concrete personification of the theological term "man in pure naturals," that is man as he was created by God before either Adam's fall or the redemption by Christ, man as he essentially is. Spenser must have had something like this in mind.

But the commentary at the beginning of canto v warns us not to push this construction too far. We have no warrant to suppose that the Salvage Man represents a stage in the history of the race. He is of gentle blood, probably the child of noble parents abandoned or stolen in infancy and brought up as Romulus and Remus were by some kindly beast. He lacks the learned characteristics of human beings, but possesses the unlearned and natural attributes of civilized human beings of the gentle classes. To Spenser heredity is as important as environment—another sign of his balanced vision of things—and the Salvage Man is morally superior to Turpine, though of course he lacks the training and experience of Calidore or Arthur. As a result of the conditions of his life he lacks much, manners in the conventional sense, even speech. His power of invincibility does not seem to have any thematic meaning.

The Salvage Man is adequate to the grave emergency when Turpine is about to kill Calepine. He watches over the wretched pair and minsters to their needs. He even knows a little folk medicine and is able to cure Calepine whose wounds are entirely physical. Serena, the victim partly of her own inadequacy and partly of the social evil, slander, he cannot cure. He protects Serena until Arthur and Timias take over this duty. The limitations of the Salvage Man appear in this scene. He would attack Arthur and Timias as he did Turpine.

The complete service of courtesy can thus be performed only by one who combines essential goodness with training, as Arthur does. This notion that virtue is compounded of intention and ability is often repeated in Spenser. The first book is its most thorough enunciation, for the difficulties in which Redcross enmeshes himself are altogether due to his lack of experience. Like the Salvage Man he cannot tell the true from the counterfeit, he cannot see Duessa beneath Fidessa. The Salvage Man has the same fundamental impulse to do good as Redcross, but in a cruder form. When he joins Arthur and Timias his good intentions pass under the guidance of knowledge and experience.

The Cannibals who capture Serena are a combination of several elements. As a narrative motif they play the part commonly assigned to

49

thieves, pirates, and barbarians in such Hellenistic romances as Tatius' *Clitipho and Leucippe*, which has a close parallel, and Apuleius' *Golden Ass*. Reports of primitive peoples in the travel literature and the beginnings of the cult of the noble savage in Montaigne's *Essay on Cannibals* enter into their composition. Mother Pauline Parker sees the Cannibals as an appropriate symbol of the after effects of Slander, which eats up its victims. Other critics have professed to see Spenser's picture of the contemporary Irish. Little but the detail of the bagpipes supports this notion, for certainly not even Spenser imputed anthropophagy or human sacrifice to the Irish. The identification has perhaps a little truth, however, notably that the Irish living at a lower social level than the English are not therefore more virtuous but less.

This is then another treatment of the primitive. The Cannibals are a maleficent aspect of the primitive, as the Satyrs of Book I are a relatively beneficent. The two groups have in common a perversion of religion. The Satyrs' religion, though false, seems to hurt no one but themselves; that of the Cannibals is radically discourteous. Nevertheless, the discourtesy of the Cannibals is more understandable, and even more admirable, than that of Briana and Turpine. In the journey upwards from the state of nature they have taken some wrong turnings.

They have, however, some virtues. The intended disposition of Serena is to be eaten. When the priest sees her, he reserves her for sacrifice, because they give their best to their god. And he is able to get them to perform the sacrifice, despite their hunger and lust. Religion, as Spenser writes, holds them in measure. In this they are far better than the Brigands who take Pastorella.

The voluptuous description of the nude Serena readied for sacrifice has, so far as I can see, no thematic significance, except perhaps to build the tension between the desires of the Cannibals and their religious duty. The nudity is a more violent repetition of Briana's custom. Serena is degraded before being killed. Of the whole incident the most obvious meaning is that discourtesy, even in its most violent forms, does not necessarily come from bad intentions. The Cannibals are in fact carrying out their most sacred duties. They are yielding their selfish desires to a tribal worship. But the religion itself, in fact their whole way of life, is essentially discourteous, for it is a complete denial of the integrity of the individual.

When the Salvage Man rescued Serena and Calepine from Turpine that was their last experience with this discourteous coward. To leave him unpunished would be to sacrifice theme to narrative. Calidore is pursuing the Blattant Beast, and so it is Arthur, the great intervener of the *Faerie Queene*, who first assumes the responsibility for Serena and then takes on the unfinished business of giving Turpine his come-uppance. Materially,

Turpine illustrates the discourtesy of refusing hospitality, which is an obligation of the high-born and well-to-do. He is also the embodiment of the bully and coward, picking a fight with Calepine when he has the advantage, but running from equal combat with Arthur. He is shifty and his word means nothing. He hires two knights to ambush Arthur, and fails to give them a true picture of their adversary.

Turpine is not unmotivated. The Porter who refuses hospitality to Calepine explains that his master is "terrible and stearne" to all errant knights "because of one, that wrought him fowle despight." The Porter gives no more information, nor does Spenser as omniscient author interrupt the narrative for an enclosed exposition. But perhaps the hint is enough if we join to it the character of Blandina. In the first meeting with Calepine and afterwards when he seeks shelter in the castle, Blandina urges hospitality on Turpine. Later, when Arthur chases Turpine into her chamber, she talks Arthur out of his disgust at Turpine's base conduct. Though her husband has been almost killed, Blandina shows no malice towards Arthur, in fact entertaining him with "courteous glee and goodly feast" when he spends the night.

Yet Spenser tells us in two stanzas of authorial omniscience that she was false and all her graces but flattery. We can scarcely regard the characterization of Blandina as fully realized or adept, but perhaps we can guess that Spenser intended us to understand that Blandina's falseness with some errant knight is what soured Turpine in the first place. Hence Turpine and Blandina are a pair to illustrate the Aristotelian defect and excess of hospitality.

The manner of Turpine's punishment deserves a word also. He is not slain, but left baffled, hung up by his heels. This is an appropriate fate for the coward and bully, disgrace rather than death. Braggadochio is somewhat similarly treated, and the comparison makes us realize that the episode of Turpine is more comic than serious. It is an application of the formula of leaving the comic villain frustrated and humiliated, but not destroyed, as, for instance, Shakespeare leaves Malvolio. If the tone is comic, the reader will understand that probably someone came along to cut Turpine down before he died, and that he never outlived his disgrace to become again a menace to errant knights. Spenser does not end the episode with a rehabilitation, as he does with Briana. Of course, the Salvage Man killed Turpine's porter and heaps of his retainers, just as Calidore had to kill Briana's seneschal before he could get into the castle. And the unnamed companion of Sir Enias has perished also. But there is, I believe, in the conventions of romance a considerable thematic difference between the deaths of minor characters and those of major ones.

The intervention of Arthur follows the pattern of Book V, in a lesser degree that of Books I and II. In the first two books Arthur has to rescue

Redcross from the results of his follies and watch over Guyon while he is unconscious. He is certainly a symbol of divine aid in both books. In Books III and IV Arthur's appearances do not seem to be a part of the thematic pattern, but, as with much else, Book V returns to a modified form of the pattern of Books I and II. The modification is that Arthur's appearance is convenient rather than strictly necessary. He does not rescue the champion but takes over part of the champion's work. In Book V after assisting Artegall in the rescue of Samient from two pagan knights and fighting Artegall by mistake until Samient stops the two of them, he joins forces with Artegall and accepts from Mercilla the task of suppressing Geroneo. This needs doing, and Artegall is already occupied with the rescue of Irena from Grantorto.

In Book VI Arthur performs essentially the same function, to take over a responsibility which the champion is unable to perform. Calidore is on the quest of the Beast; Calepine, if equal to the task of disciplining Turpine, is lost. So Arthur appears. As in Books I and II, Arthur is an exemplar of the virtue of the book. His courtesy is demonstrated in the care of Serena, the sparing of Enias, and the willingness to release Mirabella from her persecutors.

The story of Timias, however, is closer to the theme of the book than that of Arthur. Timias is more a victim of discourtesy than a champion of courtesy. In both narrative and theme Timias' adventures are a continuation of those in Book IV. Rathborne sees the love of Timias and Belphebe as platonic. A better interpretation is that it is a romance of two adolescents, developing from friendship into mature sexual love, with many ups and downs. When we leave Timias and Belphebe in Book IV the romance is on the up; when we resume it in Book VI it has turned downward.

Though Belphebe does not appear and is mentioned only once, the enclosed expository story of the attack on Timias by Despetto, Decetto, and Defetto and his being bitten by the Blattant Beast surely represents the progress of his suit to Belphebe. The three attackers, personifications of Despite, Deceit, and Detraction, who try in vain to ruin Timias, must be envious and malicious acquaintances who try to alienate Belphebe from Timias.

Failing, they call on the Blattant Beast. Timias, the huntsman, cannot resist the impulse to chase the Beast, and he puts it to flight, but not before it nips him. This must be some rash act by Timias which furnishes the basis of a campaign of slander. The three then find Timias tired by the chase and attack him and have him almost overpowered when Arthur rides up to scatter them. The infection of the Beast's bite now begins to take its toll with Timias as it has with Serena. The elements in this metaphorical account of slander are the immature person who gives a slight opening, the detractors who know that if you throw enough mud some will stick, and the purveyors of slander who seize the slightest opportunity to do their work.

The hermit to whom Arthur takes the two sufferers is another expression of experience. He has been a famous knight and knows the ways of the world from which he has retired. Spenser, though a believer in the ultimate triumph of innocence, is tough minded enough to know that the innocent suffer great harm, especially when they are young and heedless, and they need the assistance of the older and more experienced to get them out of their difficulties.

The thematic implications of the hermit's cure are clear. The narrative technique does not, however, realize the implications. Spenser has chosen to represent the effect of slander by the metaphor of an infected wound. Having made this choice, he switches from metaphor to letter in mid-career. In modern terminology, the hermit discovers that physical medicine will not cure Timias and Serena; it is a task for psychiatry, the first condition of whose success is that the patient desire to help himself. So the hermit's cure is merely the advice to stop the occasions of slander by curbing the affections. Spenser knows that you cannot stop gossips from talking; you can only give them as little as possible to talk about.

Neither Timias nor Serena profits as much as they might from the Hermit's advice. Timias' first act after his discharge is to attack Disdain and Scorn, the fool and the churl who torment Mirabella. This is comparable in rashness to Redcross' chasing Despair immediately after his release from Orgoglio's dungeon. Timias is returning to his old ways of biting off more than he can chew. Serena likewise relapses: she runs away when the fight starts.

The interwoven stories of Timias, Serena, and Mirabella have in common a concern with the applications of courtesy to love. Timias and Serena are victims of their lack of foresight, which leaves them open to the attack of slander. Mirabella has called down her own misfortune on her head by her pride. Spenser remarks that Disdain is "sib to great Orgoglio," a manner of saying that pride is Mirabella's chief vice. Born of mean parentage, her desirability has made her the reigning beauty of the moment. The adulation has gone to her head, and she makes a game of breaking hearts. She is using people, her suitors, to build up her self-esteem, just as Briana does. The inevitable reaction then sets in.

Spenser presents this scene in another metaphor, this one successful. Mirabella's willful disregard of the feelings of her admirers comes to the notice of Cupid, who indicts and tries her for crimes against courteous love. When the evidence breaks down Mirabella's stubborn pride she throws herself on the mercy of the court. Cupid "who is mild by kind" assigns her the penance of wandering about the world, tormented by

Scorn and Disdain, until she has saved as many as formerly she ruined. Timias provides her first opportunity. When his foot slips in the fight and Disdain overpowers and binds him, Mirabella's compassion goes out to him. Her entreaties are of no avail and the wretched procession, now larger by one, passes on until Arthur and Enias interrupt it.

When Enias, like Timias, falls before Disdain, Arthur has to intervene to free both Timias and Enias. As several times before in the *Faerie Queene*, Spenser endows the fight with thematic significance.* Disdain heaves up his iron baton to give Arthur a lethal blow, but Arthur ducks under, and the force of the blow throws Disdain off his balance and he cracks his leg. The meaning is clearly that Disdain, the practice of treating others as though they were dirt, defeats itself, but only when the opponent is a self-assured, toughened Arthur. To the less experienced and less assured, like Timias, Serena, and Enias, the experience of being denied all esteem is devastating.

Whether Timias profits from the experience we do not learn, but Mirabella does. When Arthur is about to take advantage of Disdain's helplessness, she saves the churl, and she also saves Scorn from being beaten to death by the Salvage Man. To Arthur's offer of release, she replies that her penance is for her own good, "least vnto me betide a greater ill." Mirabella needs the complete experience of degradation so that she will never again degrade anyone. Spenser knows that we cannot banish Disdain and Scorn from society, anymore than we can permanently muzzle slander. The only remedy in this imperfect world lies in the individual.

The narrative structure of Book VI is a little peculiar: the champion is absent from the action through the whole central part of the book, from the middle of canto iii to the beginning of canto ix. The unity of the book therefore depends on theme rather than story line. The exemplification and illustration of courtesy begun by Calidore continues with Calepine and Arthur. The episodes of Calepine and Turpine, the Salvage Man, Serena and the Cannibals, Arthur and Turpine, and Mirabella are studies of courtesy and discourtesy in action.

When Calidore returns to the story the exploration of courtesy rises to a higher, more general level, though it is still worked out in narrative, with only a little help from Spenser's commentary. One way to state the nature of this exploration is to suppose that Spenser asks two questions: First, if there could be a society all members of which are uniformly courteous, what would it be like and what would happen to it? Second, what is perfect courtesy, not in action, but in essence? Calidore's experiences in cantos ix-xi are the answers to these questions.

---

* E.g., the fight between Arthur and Pyrochles, II, viii, 48.

Canto xi opens with a summary narrative of Calidore's pursuit of the Blattant Beast, which has led Calidore through all the estates of society and classes of men. Expectably, Spenser states this spatially:

Him [the Blattant Beast] first from court he [Calidore] to the citties coursed,
And from the citties to the townes him prest
And from the townes into the countrie forsed,
And from the country back to priuate farmes he scorsed.
From thence into the open fields he fled. (ix, 3-4)

Calidore has been chasing the Beast outward and downward in society, and he now stands at Society's utmost confines, for the "open fields" are held by the humblest members, the shepherds.

Here he loses the trail when he comes on a group of shepherds who know nothing of the Blattant Beast. In fact, they know no "wicked feend that mote offend / Their happie flocks." Spenser surely does not mean that the Blattant Beast is unknown to all shepherds, that discourtesy is alien to the pastoral life, wherever practiced. These shepherds are a special group —I am tempted to call them in scientific jargon a "theoretical model" —who live outside the limits of the society we know. We have really passed into another world, a hypothetical world created by Spenser to test a hypothesis.

That this world is constructed of familiar materials, the temporal concept of perfection that places it long ago in a Golden Age or a Garden of Eden, the spatial concept (which was to dominate in the next age after Spenser's) that finds it in a remote land, and the conventions of pastoralism, ought not to blind us to its real nature. Perhaps Spenser in some moods would have accepted the notion implicit in the pastoral tradition that a perfect society would consist of shepherds. But when he faced the actual world, he created in the *Shepherd's Calender* shepherds quite unlike those of Arcady, and always present to his mind must have been the certainty that a society of actual people untouched by civilization would be like that of the Cannibals who capture Serena. Besides, Melibee, the patriarch of Arcady, has lived in the society we know. He left it.

So when Melibee entertains Calidore with a laudatory account of the simple life, he incorporates several details which gives us clues as to how we should regard this small area of perfection: "To them, that list, the worlds gay showes I leaue" he says and makes it clear that, for him at least, the life in Arcady is a result of choice. He knows all about the follies and pride of the great, how ambition drives them down to decay who might otherwise live without grief. He learned life in the discourteous world in his ten years at court:

Where I did sell my selfe for yearely hire
And in the Prince's gardin daily wrought. (ix, 24)

After ten years he cloyed of this life, recognized his mistake, and returned to Arcady.

Most commentators take the passage literally: Melibee was a gardener
at court. Melibee's description is more impressive if we take the lines as
figurative, that Melibee was a courtier, trading his freedom for a salary or
perquisites and perhaps the delusory ambition of advancement. It is not
necessary, however, to adopt this interpretation to agree that the manner
of life in Arcady is Melibee's choice. He could as easily have led the
shepherds into an emulation of courtly society—which would now be
called progress—but chose to devote himself to the preservation of the
old ways.

Why does Calidore stop? On the narrative level, it is undoubtedly the
love of Pastorella that detains him, for when he accepts the invitation of
the shepherds to rest a while, he immediately sees Pastorella, whose
beauty and manners impress him as excelling "the meane of shepheards"
so far as to be "a Prince's Paragone esteemed." This is a happy blending
of contradictions. In passing, Spenser has observed that Calidore made no
great show of rank or class "where was no need." On the other hand, the
minute he sees something good he judges it to be better than one would
expect among shepherds. In fact, like recognizes like, Calidore Pastorella
for what she is, the daughter of a famous knight and the grand daughter
of the Lord of Many Isles. The resolution is that Calidore, precisely
because he is not impressed by the outward shows of gentility, instantly
perceives its inward essence.

Can we apply thematically the narrative motif of Calidore's love at first
sight for Pastorella? I believe we can. Calidore, the exemplar of courtesy,
recognizes the essence of the virtue in the simple shepherds who have
never heard of the Blattant Beast; in Pastorella, who though lacking a
castle like Briana and Blandina is nevertheless the real female embodiment
of courtesy; in Melibee who has chosen the simple life, where lives real
courtesy, instead of the life of the court, where ambition and folly choke
it.

If this is so, we need to limit and qualify the commentary with which
Spenser begins canto x:

Who now does follow the foule *Blatant Beast*,
Whilest *Calidore* does follow that faire Mayd
Vnmyndfull of his vow and high beheast. (x, 1)

This is written from the limited point of view of one observing Calidore's
actions. From this point of view Calidore's stay in Arcady is a digression,

56

a dereliction from duty. But this is only a limited view. There is a larger pattern developing, unknown to the characters involved in it.

Calidore's stay in Arcady is strictly comparable to Redcross' visit to the House of Holiness. Calidore is a perfected knight of courtesy, as Redcross is not of Holiness, but there are still some things he must learn. He has practiced his courtesy in the world of Briana and the Knight of the Barge; he has missed some of the theoretical implications of courtesy. His instruction does not take the form of vigorous penance, but of personal involvement with Pastorella and his revelation comes on Mount Acidale. Only Calidore's experience reverses the order of Redcross': the revelation comes first, followed by the ordeal.

Calidore's experience on Mount Acidale is a sort of epiphany. Frye notes that the epiphany is the upper limit of literature. He could also have said that it is the upper limit of experience. Calidore's sight of the

> hundred naked maidens lilly white
> All raunged in a ring and dauncing in delight.

is the uppermost limit of courtesy, the realization of courtesy in its absolute form. Courtesy is a flower that grows on a lowly stalk, and its epiphany cannot be something ineffable and unspeakable, like the beatific vision of Dante. It is merely the sight of beings superior to men acting voluntarily in perfect order towards one another.

The dancing maidens, a hundred of them circling the three graces, who in turn circle Rosalind, are dancing to the piping of Colin Clout. Spenser has written himself, his mistress, and his sovereign into the scene, but it is not a piece of boasting, or even of decoration. Colin, the maidens, the graces, Gloriana are all necessary elements of the epiphany. Colin makes this quite clear in his explication to Calidore after the maidens have vanished, that is, all except his own role, which is stated only by implication.

The maidens are the servants of Venus and the daughters of Jove, mythologically, the Oceanids and the Graces. They act quite voluntarily, bestowing themselves as they will:

> For being gone, none can them bring in place,
> But whom they of them selues list so to grace. (st. 20)

Their thematic meaning as the bestowers of courtesy is also quite clear; they give all gracious gifts, says Colin,

> As comely carriage, entertainment kynde,
> Sweete semblaunt, friendly offices that bynde,
> And all the complements of curtesie. (st. 23)

This is a restatement of the commentary which Spenser inserted at the beginning of canto ii, that courtesy is a gift of Dame Nature.

These maidens, patrons of courtesy, circle around Rosalind, whom Colin refuses to identify, except that she is a country lass. Of course, this is personal with Spenser, but it is more. Rosalind is obviously Spenser's ideal of beauty. He finds it necessary to ask pardon for putting Rosalind in this spot, rather than Gloriana. The attribute, "greatest Majesty" is the real explanation. Gloriana, Elizabeth, is, whatever her virtues, the locus of sovereignty, hence of compulsion, and these maidens are not compelled.

This appears clearly in the fact that when Calidore walks up they are dancing to the piping of Colin Clout. Colin Clout is here Spenser generalized, the poet, the maker. He has made the epiphany by providing the structure of order, his piping, which impells the hundred naked maidens to subject themselves to it and to each other in a perfect expression of voluntary order, the dance. The perfect order is then a product of the imagination, of art, of a world above the practical one in which Calidore lives and acts. It is not an ideal world, in the platonic sense, but it is a world which exists only in the imagination and is accessible only to those who, like the artist, can body forth the imagined in concrete form.

Calidore sees the dancing maidens only for a little while. When they see him, they all vanish like any fairy ring. The meaning is that Calidore belongs to the practical world of men, where live the Brianas, the Turpines, the Blattant Beasts, not to the higher world of perfect social order. This world he can experience only from the outside and through a revelation. He has been trying to make it his own world by stopping in Arcady, but Arcady is an insubstantial shadow of the reality he sees on Mount Acidale. Calidore now has the answer to the second question. Courtesy is in essence the dancing maidens. This answer contains the answer to the first question. There cannot be a society of perfect courtesy; if you think you have found one, as Calidore does, you will soon find that it cannot last.

The awkward incident of the tiger can be justified as a sort of preview of what is going to happen to Arcady. We find that, despite the conviction of the shepherds, Arcady does contain a "wicked feend that mote offend / Their happie flocks." Spenser actually uses the word "feend" to describe the tiger. One could also put a similar construction on the cowardly behavior of Coridon, but I prefer to regard him as simply the stock comic rustic.

Not only is there a tiger inside Arcady, but immediately outside it are the forces of discourtesy in its most violent form, the Brigands. These are far worse than any other figures of discourtesy we have met, worse than Briana, or Turpine, or Mirabella, or even the Cannibals. They have abandoned all order, no longer living by the "plow or spade" but on spoil and booty, which they have commercialized. They sell their victims into slavery, the ultimate insult to the dignity of the individual. And they crash into Arcady, spoiling the cottages, driving away the flocks, and making captives of Coridon, Melibee, and Pastorella.

If the *Faerie Queene* were a schematic allegory on the model of Guillaume de Lorris' *Romance of the Rose*, Book VI could end here. The two major themes of the last section of the book are finished: the illusory courtesy of Arcady lies in ruin; the only real courtesy has been revealed on Mount Acidale. But the *Faerie Queene* is also romance, demanding a narrative as well as a thematic conclusion. This we get in the last two cantos, and in such a manner as to show clearly the interfusion of narrative and theme.

Earlier, we noted that the champion of courtesy always cleans up the individual problems of victims of discourtesy before resuming his pursuit of the Beast. The affair at Briana's castle and Calidore's seeing Aladine and Priscilla safely home require detours in the chase of the Beast, but if Calidore turned his back of their needs to pursue his main purpose he would hardly be the champion of courtesy. Even more necessary is the rescue of Pastorella, with whom Calidore is personally involved.

That Calidore resorts to the subterfuge of representing himself and Coridon as shepherds to the Brigands is of some thematic interest—both he and Arthur have previously used guile. And Pastorella uses it, too, in feigning an encouragement for the Captain of the Brigands which she does not feel. Though Calidore uses some force to rescue Pastorella, he relies more on guile and on the nature of the Brigands, which has given him his opportunity. As soon as they have the captives safely in prison, they fall to fighting among themselves. The Captain desires Pastorella as his own paramour, and some of the Brigands support him. Others prefer the price which the slavers will pay for her. So one kind of discourtesy, lust, cancels another, cupidity. In the fight many of the Brigands are slain, as well as Melibee and many of his people, and Pastorella is wounded. Confusion enables Coridon to escape and bring Calidore. Aided by night and his disguise Calidore makes the rescue rather easily.

To Coridon, Calidore gives the flocks the Brigands had stolen. Arcady is thus reconstituted as it should be, with a bumpkin as its leader instead of a philosopher, and deprived of its chief ornament, Pastorella. Calidore takes her to the Castle Belgard and leaves her in the care of its lord and lady, Sir Bellamoure and Lady Claribell, who are, as all readers of romance would expect, Pastorella's real parents. This completes the moral of Arcady. Pastorella is not a shepherdess by class, but only by circumstance. She is really of gentle blood, like Calidore, and fitted to be his mate. One can view this as an example of Elizabethan anti-democratic bias but it goes far deeper. It is Spenser's recognition that, after all, courtesy is the virtue of the court, most nearly though not universally realized in the upper classes of civilized society. The one solid surviving thing in the illusion of Arcady is Pastorella, who didn't belong there at all.

With Pastorella settled and safe, Calidore can complete his quest. Spenser resumes the chase of the Blattant Beast "through all estates,"* coming at last to the clergy. "At last" because the clergy should by profession be more immune to the Beast than the laity, and of the clergy, the monks should be the most immune. The havoc the Beast works among the clergy, especially the monks, can be interpreted two ways: that the clergy have been innocent victims of slander; or that the spirit of slander pervades and perverts the clergy, especially the monks. At first thought, one naturally supposes that Spenser intended the latter meaning, and so the passage becomes a conventional Protestant satire on the Old Church. The mention of the "filth and ordure" which the Beast finds in the monks' cells supports this interpretation, but the other shines through, and probably Spenser intended it so, for there is more than one evidence of nostalgia for the Old Church in the *Faerie Queene*.

The final conquest of the Beast is an anticlimax, if one expects something like the struggle between Redcross and the Old Dragon. Since the Beast is presented at the opening of Book VI as a supernatural monster, offspring of Cerberus and Chimera fostered in "Stygian fen," such an expectation would seem natural. But this is not what we have actually been working up to. All the way through the book the Beast has inflicted its injury hit-and-run on the weak, the unprepared, and the inept. When Calidore finally bays it, Spenser immediately cuts the Beast down to size in a simile comparing it to a bullock felled by "butchers balefull hand." Thereafter though "he grind, hee bit, he scratcht, he venim threw," he is not really dangerous. Either Spenser has made a mistake, or he means that slander, even discourtesy generally, is only an evil by estimation. It cannot harm the strong and the alert. These need fear it no more than Calidore does.

Calidore muzzles the Beast, leads it through Fairyland in triumph, finally chains it up where it can presumably never do any more harm. But it eventually breaks loose again, "whether wicked fate so framed / Or fault of men." At least one critic has blamed Sir Calidore for chaining the Beast "so insecurely that the monster succeeds in regaining his liberty." Surely this is a misunderstanding of Spenser's meaning. It was not Calidore's ineptness that liberated the Beast, but the human condition. The Beast can no more remain chained than Arcady can last. The victory of virtue is personal and temporary. In fact the "wicked fate" that allows

---

* "Estates" is purposefully ambiguous: "possessions" and "conditions of life."

the Beast to break his iron chain is "the fault of men." After all, it was Pyrochles who, after Guyon had bound Furor and Occasion, demanded their release and was their next victim (II, v). This is the tough-minded Spenser speaking, the man who had understood the world well enough to know that the Beast will always ramp through society, despite the efforts of Sir Calidore, Sir Pelleas, Sir Lamorack, or even Edmund Spenser.

Name and Character

ANY INQUIRY into character and characterization in the *Faerie Queene* must begin with the question whether the poem has any characters. Since it is narrative, the work required historiae personae, personages, named individuals who perform actions, but are they characters? Certainly the traditional manner of speaking about literary characters, that they are "realistic," seem "drawn from the life," are "round" rather than "flat," and the like seems as inappropriate to the *Faerie Queene* as it would to Grimm's Fairy Tales.

The main reason is not that Spenser's creations are all good or all bad, all right or all wrong, mere counters in a game. Spenser's personages are not that, as one might think from a superficial acquaintance with the work. They are not naive, apparent, or unsubtle. The difficulty is quite different: it is simply that most of our norms, most of the received doctrine concerning character and characterization is directed towards the drama, especially tragedy, and the novel, especially the social novel. And they do not seem to fit the mixed genre of the *Faerie Queene*, combined as it is of elements of romance, personification-allegory, pastoral, and even epic.

Perhaps if the work were entirely romance the task of analyzing character would be simpler. The personages of romance are historical in the wider sense that myth and legend are included in history. The chief characters of the two romance patterns Spenser follows most closely, the Italian and the Arthurian, are all presumably historical. Charlemagne and Orlando, Arthur and Merlin at least began their literary careers in works offered to the readers as history. Invented personages, of which there are many in each type of romance, were fitted into a quasi-historical framework, just as Siegfried and Beowulf, obviously gods or heroes out of myth, are fitted into historical events.

The same holds true for tragedy, as practiced, for instance, by Shakespeare. Some of his tragedies are actually chronicle plays, *Richard II* and *Richard III*. Others come from recognized historical sources, *Lear* from Holinshed, *Hamlet* ultimately from Saxo Grammaticus, and *Julius Caesar* from Plutarch. Even the private or domestic tragedies, *Romeo* and *Othello*, come from collections that purport to be reports of actual happenings. In the Elizabethan phrase they are "true histories."

Romance, in one or another of its many forms, set most of the patterns for fiction. The numbers of romances that entertained Elizabethans, whether of the higher sort like *Arcadia* or the lower like *Jack of Wilton*, all purported to be "true histories," and especially in the lower form they pretty well decided the development of the novel as it appears in *Tom Jones* or *Pamela*. The point is not that *Tom Jones* is more historical, in the sense of being closer to actual events, than the *Faerie Queene*, but that in one important element it seems to be. Its personages (that is most of them) bear names actually borne by human beings in the past or similar to those borne by human beings in the present. The incidents, likewise, are in their details such as happen in our experience. The elements of design and artifice which bear witness to authorial tampering with impersonal fact are neither more nor less present in *Hamlet* or *Tom Jones* than in the *Faerie Queene*. What matters is that the personages, Hamlet and Claudius, Tom Jones and Squire Western, bear names which are only conventional references whereas Calidore, Serena, Blandina are names capable of understanding as common nouns or adjectives. The name Tom Jones tells one nothing about the nature of the personage; the name Calidore tells us much.

Spenser's practice in giving a great number of his characters names of intrinsic, as against conventional, meaning is explicable on three levels, a genetic, a philosophical, and an artistic. Genetically, the *Faerie Queene* derives from two strains of literature, its narrative method from romance, its method of handling personages from the personification-allegory, as exemplified by the morality plays and, above all, the *Romance of the Rose*.*

This is, I believe, what Spenser means by stating in the first sentence of the Letter to Ralegh that the *Faerie Queene* is an "allegory, or dark conceit," and then a few lines later an "historical fiction," and, in another few lines, a historical poem, and thereafter seemingly vacillating between allegory and history. Spenser sharply differentiates between the methods of the "poet historical" and the "historiographer." He is hence under no illusion that his work is what we would call historical, i.e., a report on actual personages and occurrences. History to him means "narrative," the aspect of the word which became "story." And by emphasizing about equally "allegory" and "history" he shows his awareness of the combination of methods, the romance method in the narrative, and the personification-allegory method in the personages, characteristic of the *Faerie Queene*.

Spenser's choice was partially dictated by, or at least conformable to, a philosophical position, the one initially espoused by Socrates in Plato's *Cratylus*. Of all the doctrines of Plato the one on the nature and origin of language developed in the *Cratylus* is the most alien to contemporary

---

* Despite the name I do not mean to include the *Romance of the Rose* under the category of romance; it is a personification allegory.

thought. It is simply that language is not at all conventional, that each word carries within it, entirely apart from the conventions of reference, its own meaning. Thus, in one example Socrates gives, man is called ἄνθροπος because he is the only creature that looks up, considers what he sees, he is ὁ ἀναθρῶν ἃ ὄπωπεν.

It is possible that this is satire, that Socrates is reducing the methods of the Sophists to absurdity, but it was taken seriously for more than a thousand years. In the Christianized version, the action of Adam in naming the animals is giving them names which contained, often cryptically, a statement of their natures. Augustine and Jerome among the fathers make much use of Plato's methods, extending them, of course, to Latin and Hebrew. The practice of etymology as seen in Isidore of Seville is based on Plato's theory. Hardly a commentator on Genesis of Spenser's century omits a quotation or reference to the *Cratylus* in his exegesis of Genesis 2:20. Spenser himself obviously accepted the practice, as when he makes a point of deriving "courtesy" from "court," (i, 1) which justifies his selection of all his models of courtesy from among courtiers. In Book I he specifically applies the practice of etymology to the naming of characters:

His name *Ignaro* did his nature right aread. (viii, 31)

The artistic effect produced by following the theory of Plato and the practice of the morality play clearly differs from the more representational method of tragedy, the Italian romances, and the "realistic" novel. In these forms we first confront what seems to be a "true history," a report or representation of actual events and personages. The personages seem to us to be human beings as we know them, with perhaps minor differences owing to place, time, level of society, and the like. It is only later, after acquaintance with a large body of such literature, after arriving at some sophistication in our taste, that we begin recognizing elements of design and form which are quite unrepresentative of what we accept as "ordinary life." Both *Huckleberry Finn* and *Tom Jones* turn out to be quests and so to find kinship with the *Quest of the Holy Grail* and the *Epic of Gilgamesh*. Likewise Ibsen's *Ghosts* and O'Neill's *Desire Under the Elms* share with *Oedipus* the motifs of incest and ancestral curse.

This sort of surprise, the discovery of universality in individuality, of pattern in chaos, is perhaps one of the prime pleasures of literature. It is not, however, the one that Spenser chose for his readers. He approached the matter from the opposite end and reversed the surprise. As a setting for his work he chose fairyland, where happen events outside ordinary experience, performed by personages named and motivated differently from those on our level of existence. He would seem to be doing everything possible to prevent identification of his personages and events with those familiar to us from experience. And yet he tells us in the Letter to Ralegh that his purpose is to fashion a gentleman, not an angel or a fairy or any sort of other-world creature, but a gentleman.

He does, and this is his reverse surprise. We find individuality in universality, diversity in pattern, the ordinary in the exotic. This phenomenon happens perhaps oftener in Book VI than elsewhere, but examples are found in every book. One is the Aladine-Priscilla-Knight of the Barge episode. Remove the fairyland setting, correct for time, and the narrative becomes as much a part of our experience as a story in yesterday's newspaper: two teen-agers parked on a lonely road and victimized by a psychopathic "love bandit." The ease with which one makes such translations is a testimony to the universality of Spenser's artistic conception and the success of his tactics.

In the more representational forms, tragedy and the novel, personages start as individuals and achieve generality, start as entities and get names, and the names start empty of meaning and achieve meaning. But most of Spenser's personages start as names, figures of speech or generalizations and through the process of narrative achieve individuality and personality. Narrative thus makes personages into characters.

The proper place to begin the analysis of a Spenserian personage is then with the name. Though it is not true that Spenser pursued an absolutely consistent scheme in naming his characters, his habits and preferences are visible enough to permit a rough categorization of the names he gives his characters. These categories are rather points along a continuum than discrete bins. There are four such points: (1) personifications in English (Disdain or Scorn), or in some foreign language (Despetto, Decetto, Defetto); (2) "cues," in which the etymology gives a cue to the nature or function of the personage; (3) conventional proper names, apparently empty of intrinsic meaning, often of a historical or literary personage (Arthur), or a common Christian name (Matilda) and finally; (4) some characters having no names but called by their functions or characteristics (Salvage Man, the Hermit). Since these are points rather than bins, there are some characters with names falling between the points (Timias, Briana), and it is entirely possible that we have lost the clue that would enable us to understand some others.

Book VI has only four personages who are pure English personifications, all of them in the Mirabella episode. Infamy and Despite appear only briefly as witnesses at the inquest which indicts Mirabella. Their appearance is confined to three lines and their only action is to give evidence that Cupid's missing followers have been betrayed by Mirabella, an action which only personifies the results of Mirabella's behavior. To say that Infamy and Despite testify against Mirabella is merely a figurative way of saying that she has got a bad name (infamy) and incurred the enmity (despite) of many people, who now act to punish her.

Disdain and Scorn have larger parts. They are the churl and the fool who accompany Mirabella on her penance. Disdain leads her horse; Scorn mocks her. As with Infamy and Despite, the actions of Disdain and Scorn are mere exemplifications of the attitudes or qualities that give them their names. The difference between the two sets of personages is that Disdain and Scorn each perform several actions and are involved in reactions and interactions with other personages. When we first see them they are frozen figures in a tableau. When Timias attempts to intervene the tableau explodes into action. Disdain chases Timias and when Timias loses his footing, beats him down, binds him, and leads him, while the fool Scorn whips and reviles him.

This series of actions is substantially repeated when Sir Enias attacks Disdain. Enias, too, is beaten and about to be bound, when Arthur attacks to rescue his squire and his companion. Disdain turns Enias over to Scorn and meets Arthur's onslaught. When Disdain heaves up his huge club to drive Arthur into the earth, Arthur slips under the blow, hits Disdain in the knees, and is about to finish him off, when Mirabella pleads for his life.

The main actions of Disdain and Scorn are exemplifications of the abstract qualities they personify, but not quite every detail can be so explained: why, for instance, does Arthur hit Disdain in the knee, not elsewhere? And the action advances a little beyond simple personification in the cooperation of Disdain and Scorn in binding Enias. Disdain alone binds Timias, which may mean that Disdain so humiliates a person that he is rendered incapable of action. When, however, Scorn and Disdain act together this is the first advance of a personification in the direction of becoming an individualized character.

Spenser is, of course, doing nothing unusual in making such an advance. Personifications inevitably tend to develop individuality and become real characters. Piers Plowman is full of examples, of which the best known is perhaps the sketch of Gluttony in the confession of the seven deadly sins (B text, passus v). In the morality *Mankind*, the personages, in spite of bearing such names as Mercy, Mankind, Nought, Newguise, become individualized characters. But such a complete transformation of personification into character never, I believe, happens in the *Faerie Queene*. A step or two in that direction is all Spenser permits himself.

This generalization will apply as well to the personifications whose names are not English, but foreign or quasi-foreign. Perhaps there is no real difference whether you label a personage Pride or Orgueil, except in the distance between the reader and the action narrated. Pride is slightly closer to an abstraction than is Orgueil. Moreover, it appears that Spenser did not always regard the two classes as separate, for he says that Disdain was "sib to Orgoglio." Despetto, Decetto, and Defetto, the three enemies of Timias who lure him to chase the Blattant Beast and when he is wounded attack him and beat him down until he is rescued by Arthur, are obviously sib to Despite, Deceit, and Defect. In fact, they are merely Italianizations of these words—not really Italian, for standard Italian would call for Dispetto and Difetto. I have not found such a form as Dicetto.

These are all the true personifications found in Book VI. None plays a very extensive part in the story. In fact, all are found in enclosed narratives of past actions used as exposition. In playing relatively minor roles these personages resemble the personifications in other parts of the *Faerie Queene*, where characteristically they are limited to set pieces like the pageant of the seven deadlies in Book I, the banquet of the three sisters, Elissa, Perissa, and Medina in Book II, and the trial of Duessa before Mercilla in Book V. Nowhere do they go farther towards becoming real characters. Book VI makes even less use of personifications than the earlier books. The reason is the middle flight which designedly it flies. Just as Book VI avoids the full romance mode of narrative with its other-world magic, so it also eschews personification.

Book VI is exceptional in the *Faerie Queene* for both the proportion and the importance of personages bearing cue names. Both the champion and the anti-champion belong in this category, Calidore and the Blattant Beast. Of the other books, only Four has one of its two champions, Triamond, with a cue name. Elsewhere, Guyon and Britomart are pure names, one of a mortal the other of a goddess. Cambell seems a pure name also, Artegall, apparently a combination of Arthur and Galles, a made-up name, to be placed between the cue name and the pure name. The Red Cross Knight is, strictly speaking, nameless; or perhaps we should think of him as St. George. Anti-champions, adversaries of the champions and representatives of evil, frequently bear cue names: Duessa, Acrasia, Malecasta, Archimago, Cymochles, Pyrochles; the list is long.

The thematic and affective use Spenser makes of his champion's names in Book VI is also possibly unique in the *Faerie Queene*. Calidore, "beautiful gift," is a nutshell definition of courtesy, which Spenser tells us early in the book is a gift of Nature, who makes some "so goodly gratious by kind," that their every action pleases, whereas others who have "greater skill in mind" cannot attain the perfection which Calidore has by nature. The ease that comes of natural aptitude plus experience appears in every act of Calidore, and of Arthur as well, when he takes over the position of champion in Calidore's absence through the middle part of the book.

The Blattant Beast is a parallel abstract of discourtesy. I follow Leslie

67

Hotson in supposing that the name comes from βλάπτω, which for euphony Spenser has changed to βλάττω, and I have therefore used the spelling "blattant," found only twice in the 1596 text, as probably more representative that "blatant" of what Spenser intended in sound and etymology. The great Greek dictionary of Stephanus (Estienne), which was authoritative for Spenser's generation, gives no such form as βλάττω, but the assimilation of ππ to ττ is not uncommon, and Spenser would not have been misunderstood by the reader with a modicum of Greek. Stephanus derives βλάπτω from βλάβη which he defines as "noxia, detrimentum, damnus," harm, damage, injury.

The name is thus a cue to the personage, if one can call a beast a personage. The Blattant Beast is merely the essential evil of slander, indeed of all discourtesy: it hurts someone. The creature's beasthood seems to be that of a dog, especially since its parent is Cerberus, but in many of its actions the Beast resembles a wild boar rather more than a dog. Most probably Spenser modeled the creature on the dragonopede, the mythical tailed, footed, and winged beast which figures so prominently in medieval art as a symbol of evil. In one version of the Orpheus and Eurydice story, which may have provided the inspiration for the biting of Serena, the text says that Eurydice is bitten by a serpent, but the illustrations show a dragonopede.

Of the large number of personages in Book VI, some have such brief walk-on's that we can say nothing except that their names are not inappropriate. The summoner who serves Cupid's capias on Mirabella is Portamore because he carries things for the God of Love. In naming Pastorella's parents, Bellamoure and Claribell Spenser seems insisting on the elements of beauty, love, and clarity.

The seneschal who carries out Briana's orders to cut the beards off knights and the hair off their ladies is Maleffort, a name implying the misdirection of Briana's love. The giant Cormorant, whom Sir Bruin conquered, obviously takes his name from the bird, which to Elizabethans was a symbol of greediness. Although none of these names can be said to be a real clue to the nature of the individuals because they do not play large enough roles to have real natures instead of functions, still they illustrate the economy of Spenser's onomastic method, whereby the author can say so much about the personage while seeming to say so little. For instance, this is all Spenser tells us about Cormorant:

> Sir *Bruin*, who is Lord
> Of all this land, late conquer'd by his sword
> From a great Gyant, called *Cormoraunt*,
> Whom he did ouerthrow by yonder foord
> And in three battailes did so deadly daunt,
> That he dare not returne for all his daily vaunt. (iv, 29)

In this space, entirely by selection of a name, Spenser has managed to imply that Cormorant was a greedy, ugly giant, who awaits his chance to swoop down like a bird of prey and regain his possessions.

Such economy is not of course necessary with personages who have larger roles, such as Crudor, Turpine, and Blandina. The meanings of these names are pretty apparent. Crudor answers to every meaning of the Latin word *crudus*, unrefined, raw, immature. Turpine, from *turpis* or *turpo*, suggests a range of undesirable characteristics: ugly, repulsive, base, foul, infamous. His wife, Blandina, from *blandus*, flattering, seductive, illustrates flattery and soft speech, in her entertainment of Arthur, for instance. In developing her character, however, Spenser has perhaps relied too much on the name and not enough on appropriate action.

"Mirabella" seems to emphasize the wondrous beauty which by bringing her so many suitors and so much attention turned her head and made her incur the wrath of Cupid. Priscilla, though a common name borne by a saint and derived from a Roman cognomen, probably also includes the meaning of the common adjective *priscus*, "fresh." The name of her companion, Aladine, and that of his father, Aldus, probably indicate their station in life. An *allodium*, the etymon of names like Alden and most probably of Aladine and Aldus, is according to the *Oxford English Dictionary* an "estate held in absolute ownership without service or acknowledgement of any superior." In other words, Aladine and his father belong to the class of small freeholders, not to the nobility that held as tenants of a superior lord or the King. Aladine's station in life is the motivation for the incident: Priscilla's parents want a better match for her than the son of a freeholder, and so the two youngsters have to meet on the sly.

The two heroines of the book, Pastorella and Serena, both have names with an ironic twist. Pastorella's name derives from the French *pastourelle*, used as an ornamental equivalent of *bergère*, for instance in de Baif's *Eclogue XVIII*, a dialogue between "le pastoreau" and "la pastourelle." It is significant that Spenser's personification of the shepherdess is not by birth and nature a shepherdess at all, but the daughter of a knight and a lady. The pastoral life she embodies dissolves in the raid of the Brigands. Her name thus ironically supports the thematic purpose of Calidore's stay among the shepherds.

Serena's name is at first sight a complete contradiction to her nature. She is the fleeing maiden, like Florimell in Books III and IV, usually in some strait and often complaining about it. Neither her temperament nor her history is serene. The probable explanation of this contradiction is that Spenser is practicing a favorite etymological trick of the time, the etymology *lucus a non lucendo*, in which things are named for their opposites, as *lucus*, a shady grove, because it is not *lucendo*, shining. This is not quite so perverse as it seems, for we are still prone to bestow on three hundred pounders nicknames like "Tiny." As a method of naming it apparently had some attraction to Spenser. There is no other satisfactory explanation why he should have bestowed on his warrior maiden Britomart a name borne in mythology by the fleeing maiden. The effect in both instances is a humor apparent only to the initiate.

Serena's lover, Calepine, bears perhaps the most puzzling name in the book. It is an unusual name, found so far as I can discover elsewhere only as an Italian family name, Calepine. Borne by a fifteenth-century friar and compiler of a Latin dictionary, the name entered the Italian language with the meaning "Latin dictionary," whence it was apparently borrowed by French with the meaning "notebook." This etymology, however, hardly seems to fit Spenser's character. One would rather suspect that the first syllable of Calepine like that of Calidore, is the Greek καλός "beautiful." But if so, what is the rest? Certainly not πίνω "drink." Alice Blitch suggests πίνος as the second element, because Calepine's character is ambivalent. He is brave one minute, cowardly the next. Since I read Calepine's action as the result of inexperience, rather than cowardice, I find this explanation had to accept, but it has the value of expressing the inconsistency of Calepine's actions. Mother Pauline Parker apparently accepts ἔπος "speech" as the last element, for she writes that the name suggests "that he represents the sweetness of speech which is certainly a part of courtesy." This is the best of the possibilities I have discovered. There is nothing inherently improbable or contrary in it, but it is not specially appropriate either. Calepine does not exemplify sweetness of speech in any notable way, as Calidore does.

Perhaps it would be best to include Calepine in the small group of names for which we have no clue, so that we cannot be certain whether they are cues or merely empty names. Other such names are Timias and Enias, Briana and Sir Bruin, and Matilde. Some scholars have been sure that Timias derives from τίμη fame, but the thematic connection is hard to see, unless one supposes that Timias is Sir Walter Ralegh, a hypothesis that raises more questions than it answers. For Enias we have little clue in the action. He is an errant knight, deceived by Turpine into attacking Arthur, who after learning the truth joins Arthur. The name could be a variant of Aeneas. It could also come from ἐνία glossed by Stephanus as "halter" or "bridle" with a quotation from Plato in which the word is used metaphorically to mean "government" or "restraint." With an ethical implication of government of the passions or the like, it would be a suitable name, but the episode in which Sir Enias takes part has no obvious ethical import. Perhaps the further adventures which Spenser planned for him would have cleared up the meaning of the name.

Briana's name appears to be the common Irish name Brian or Brien, perhaps with the implication that the rather barbarous lack of sensitivity which she exhibits is characteristic of the Irish. Her effort to weave a mantle of the beards of knights and the tresses of ladies has an element of Celtic fantasy about it. It is entirely possible also that Spenser knew and accepted some etymology of Brian unknown to us.

With Sir Bruin we can follow the process whereby etymology becomes name. In the *View of Ireland* Spenser notes that the name Mac-Mahon means "son of the bear," because the clan is descended from an Anglo-Norman family named FitzUrsula. The totemistic appropriateness of the name to the incident is obvious: Sir Bruin is provided with an heir when Calepine rescues the babe from the mouth of a bear and gives it to Matilde, Sir Bruin's childless wife. The name Matilda was borne by several historical personages, among them the mother of Henry II of England. In romance it is the name of Rinaldo's nurse in Tasso's *Girusalame liberata*. None of those, however, seem to have any bearing on Spenser's personage. Matilde seems to be almost, if not entirely, unique among the names in Book VI. Unless the real explanation is that we have lost the clue, it is empty of both etymological meaning and association. For it has no associations or references, as do such names as Arthur, Tristram, Coridon. This is the next category of Spenserian onomastics: those with historical or literary associations.

A bridge from the etymological names to the associational ones is perhaps provided by Melissa, the old servant of Bellamoure and Claribell who nursed Pastorella as a baby and recognizes her as a woman. Though the word means simply "bee," it is doubtful if Spenser was content with such simplicity. In addition to the sweetness of honey, he probably had in mind also the sweetness of sound ($\mu\acute{\epsilon}\lambda os$ song), and possibly the action of caring for someone ($\mu\acute{\epsilon}\lambda\omega$ to be an object of care). It may well be, too, that he saw a mythological reference, for Thomas Cooper describes Melissa as "a woman who with her sister Amalthea" nursed Zeus.* A concurrence of etymology and mythological reference is a serendipity of which Spenser would naturally take advantage. And the outrageous humor of giving Pastorella and Zeus the same nurse is quite in his style, also.

All the associational names in Book VI come from two sources, Arthurian romance and Graeco-Roman pastoral. The character and function of Prince Arthur has been developed by Spenser in the Letter to Ralegh and through five books; it is not changed in Book VI. Pelleas and Lamorack play extremely minor roles, being mentioned in only one stanza (39) of the last canto as knights who pursued the Blattant Beast after he broke the iron chain with which Calidore bound him. Both names probably came to Spenser from Caxton's version of Malory. All

---

* The more usual account gives Zeus three nurses, of whom two, Adrasteia and Io, are daughters of Melisseus. The third is Amlathea.

Spenser needed was names which, though otherwise relatively neutral, would evoke Arthurian connotations, and Pelleas and Lamorack serve this use.

Tristram is another matter. The story of Tristram can hardly have been unfamiliar to any reader of the *Faerie Queene*. Many would even be familiar with the etymology proffered there, from *triste homme*. Yet the nephew of King Mark and the lover of Bele Isoud seems little kin to the young squire who slays the Knight of the Barge. The only points of contact are the parentage, which Spenser borrows from Caxton-Malory, though changing the details of Tristram's birth and enfance; and Tristram's skill in hunting. Here the resemblance ceases. In fact, the actions of Tristram show him to be modeled on another romance character, Percival, especially as he appears in the *Perlesvaus*. Why Spenser named him Tristram is not apparent.

The two pastoral names have clear references. Melibee seems to come directly from Vergil's First Eclogue, where he is a dispossessed farmer lamenting his loss and the exile it entails. To be dispossessed is, of course, also the fate of Spenser's Melibee, though he is not permitted the luxury of mourning. If one could suppose that Spenser's memory has slipped a bit and confused Meliboeus with the other speaker in the eclogue, the "lucky old man Tytyrus," the association would be complete. This, however, does not seem likely, for Tityrus is Spenser's name for Chaucer and must have been pretty well fixed in Spenser's mind. The etymology of Melibee in μελιβοή, "honey tone" according to Stephanus, or its connection with the earth goddess Meliboea or the cities named after her do not seem implied in Spenser's use of the name, nor does Chaucer's *Tale of Melibee*.

The shepherd Corydon derives from both Theocritus and Vergil. In the Fourth Idyl of Theocritus he is a cowherd, tending the herd of Aegon in the place of the regular herdsman who is competing in the Olympics. In Vergil's Second Eclogue, he appears in another role, the rejected and dejected lover who ultimately resolves to find "another Alexis." Spenser has combined both roles in his shepherd.

The onomastic practices we have been analyzing apply not only to personages but also to groups and places. The Cannibals are certainly named allusively and the Brigands possibly so. It is virtually certain that Spenser did not mean by "cannibal" only "eater of human flesh." Eaters of human flesh appear frequently in the travel literature of the middle ages and the sixteenth century, always under the title of "anthropophagi." The word "cannibal" was first used by Columbus and wherever it appears means what he meant, the Carib Indians: "Here Ruy Diaz Solis had been eaten, with some of his companions, by the anthropophagi, whom the Indians call Cannibals." The word Brigand was well on its way to becoming a common noun, but dictionaries preserved the memory that this too was originally a name of a specific people. Thomas Cooper defines Brigantes as "an ancient people in the North Part of England," not just bandits and raiders but apparently Scots bandits and raiders.

The place named Mount Acidale is obviously of mythological origin, a fairly uncommon origin for the names of Book VI. But as the vision on Mount Acidale is not a normal achievement of courtesy—it vanishes almost at once when Calidore looks—a mythological name is quite appropriate. In choosing the name Spenser doubtless had in mind the information available in such places as Cooper's dictionary, where Acidalia is defined as a "surname of Venus" and Acidalius as a "wel in Orchomenum dedicated unto Venus and the Graces."

Not all of the personages who appear in the *Faerie Queene* are named. There are many nameless ones, not all of them minor. The list of nameless personages in Book VI includes the Knight of the Barge, his lady, the Salvage Man, the Hermit, Turpine's porter, the priest of the Cannibals, and the captain of the Brigands. Some of them are nameless for obvious reasons. Lacking the power of speech, the Salvage Man could hardly communicate his name if he had one. In origin he is the "wild man," "wodewose," "homosilvester" of medieval lore, a creature whose roots lie alike in Graeco-Roman and in Germanic mythology. He is ambiguously natural and supernatural. As a natural creature he may be an abandoned human infant who survived in the wild, or he may be an adult driven out of human society by his own madness or for his crimes. As a supernatural creature he is a vegetation deity, a demon breaking out into bursts of fury. Spenser's Salvage Man has some supernatural characteristics: his invincibility, his skill with medicine (he heals Calepine's wounds by herbs) and his use of an uprooted tree as a weapon, but he is dominantly natural, apparently the abandoned child of noble parents, who has somehow survived in the forest. Mostly he is a benign creature, though traces of demonic malignancy remain in the fury with which he assails Turpine and his retainers—he would have assailed Arthur and Timias with equal fury, had Serena not restrained him.

We have observed that, although Spenser frequently introduces his characters by authorial intervention, he often does so at a time and place when it would be natural for the personages in the scene to learn the name of the newcomer. As long as Enias and Arthur are fighting or Enias is helping Arthur baffle Turpine, Enias remains nameless. Only after Turpine is baffled do we learn his name. In other words, Spenser waits for a place when the action is slow enough to permit the amenities before introducing the name. This name principle would explain why the Knight of the Barge, the priest of the Cannibals, and the captain of the Brigands remain unnamed. There is no convenient time or manner in which one of the principals, Calidore, Serena, Pastorella, could learn the name.

For Turpine's porter the function serves as well as the name. One might, however, inquire why Briana's seneschal is named (Maleffort), when Turpine's porter is not. The two are about equal in importance and their actions are similar. Perhaps it is a trivial question. But there is an explanation: Calidore learns Maleffort's name from an intermediary, the squire whom he finds tied up, whereas we have no intermediary between Arthur and Turpine's porter. Hence the difference may well reflect a possibly unconscious preference by Spenser to leave unnamed those whose names cannot be learned in a natural manner.

There could be no natural manner of learning the Hermit's name unless he gave it, and the whole purpose of being a hermit is to submerge one's identity in one's function. We learn that he was a great knight—he could easily have divulged this much about himself—but his wordly anonymity is preserved.

Premise and Anti-Premise

UNDERLYING THE *Faerie Queene* are several supporting premises, the understanding of whose existence, nature, and function is necessary to the appreciation of the intellectual structure of the whole. Such, for instance, are the beliefs that everything was better in former ages and that virtue is more abundant in the higher than in the lower classes. Explicit in many passages in all parts of the poem and implicit just about everywhere, these two premises are so fundamental that the whole thematic structure would collapse without their support. Unless they are true why would a poet intending to fashion a gentleman use a fable whose time is the Arthurian age and whose exemplary personages are knights and ladies?

No critic of the *Faerie Queene* would doubt the existence of these entities. I have just called them "premises" and "beliefs." I could also have called them "propositions," since they are reducible to propositional form. Others have used the words "motif," "image," and "idea." Any of these terms does well enough for practical purposes, but all are also used for other entities somewhat different in nature and scope. For myself, I should prefer restricting "image" to something smaller in scope, more affective, and less paraphrasable. A motif is similarly limited in scope and may be either narrative or thematic. An idea, on the other hand, cannot be narrative and cannot be used as a metaphor.

Spenser's use of the common beliefs that antique time had more virtue than modern time and that people of gentle birth are more virtuous than those of low birth has a degree of obliquity and transference which requires us to add some specification to the word "premise." Though we can state the beliefs as premises, they do not always function logically in the poem. They become metaphors. For Spenser does not believe that some specific group of men in a definite past era were more virtuous than any men are today. Or rather, he may have believed this proposition, but it is not necessary for us to believe it to make the poem function, any more than we must accept a physical hell inside the earth to make Dante's *Inferno* meaningful.

In fact, the rigorous logical application of these premises would get us into contradictions. Spenser twice asserts that the court and person of Elizabeth I are the equals of anything antiquity can show, but this cannot be if the premise is true in a logical sense. Nor can Melibee be superior in virtue to Turpine, if gentle people are more virtuous than the common folk. Moreover, one can always appeal to fact to destroy the validity of a premise. But you cannot disprove Spenser's premises of antiquity or

75

gentility by appeal to facts, for there are none. His antiquity is ideal, not actual. The superiority of Arthurian manners to Elizabethan is the superiority of the Platonic idea to its realization in matter, or, in a favorite figure of the age, the greater the purity of the water the nearer it is to its source. Indeed, Spenser indicates the nature of his premise by the use of such words as "nursery," "pattern," and "well spring."

Finally, if further proof is needed that the antiquity in which the *Faerie Queene* is laid is not chronological time but ideal timelessness, consider how easily the personages of the poem can be topical. Though the best informed current criticism rejects most of the historical identifications made in past generations, still enough remain to show the possibility: Duessa certainly is modelled on Mary Queen of Scots in the trial before Mercilla (V, ix, 40-50), and Calidore's chase of the Blattant Beast (VI, xii, 23-35) certainly contains allusions to the dissolution of the monasteries under Henry VIII.

The term "premise" must then be taken in a specialized sense: a propositional statement which serves as a basis for metaphor rather than for deductive reasoning. The premise stands midway between idea and image, statement and figure, and looks in both directions. Of course, Spenser was probably quite unconscious of all this complexity; he was doing what any good poet unconsciously does, making an idea into a metaphor.

Whether the term I have suggested is acceptable is not so important. It is only important that the reader understand the nature, function, and capability for development of these entities. Like premises they are capable of straightforward, propositional statement:

> But in the triall of true curtesie
> Its now so farre from that, which then it was
> That it indeed is nought but forgerie. (proem, st. 5)

This comes from the proem to Book VI, a section that is entirely commentary. Generally such statements do come in commentary, most often at the opening of a book or a canto.

These premises have long histories and involve many corollaries. The premise of antiquity, which sees the course of human history as a downward path from original perfection to present degeneration, is a comprehensive illustration. It has roots in both the Semitic and the Hellenic components of western culture, in the Garden of Eden and the golden age. By Spenser's time it had a history of three thousand years or so and had developed such interesting corollaries as the superiority of Hebrew-based Christianity to Greek paganism because Moses lived long before Homer, and the inferiority of rimed verse to unrimed. In some measure all this development is latent in Spenser's use of the premise. Not all

76

Spenser's premises have such venerable ancestry or so abundant a progeny, but all have ancestry and progeny.

The premise of antiquity, which is perhaps the most important one for the whole of the *Faerie Queene*, is rather sparsely represented in Book VI, explicitly in the proem and implicitly in the account of the Blattant Beast's remaining chained "long after this" until he breaks loose and, despite the efforts of Sir Pelleas and Sir Lamorack, "raungeth through the world againe." For the rest, the premise manifests its presence principally in the fact that the action belongs to "timeless, wavering myth," rather than to history. In essence, that is what Spenser's antiquity is, the timeless era before time began, in which absolute form has its home.

More important to Book VI than antiquity is gentility: that the highest virtue is found only in those of gentle birth. As against the premise of antiquity, which occurs mainly in the commentary, that of gentility pervades the whole book of courtesy. Clearly, to Spenser courtesy is possible only to the well born. Book VI begins with the assertion that courtesy derives its name from the court:

> For that it there most vseth to abound
> And well beseemeth that in Princes hall
> That virtue should be plentifully found. (i, 1)

Spenser does not mean that courtesy ought to be found in a court, but that in its perfection it must be found there or nowhere. It is plain that courtesy, no matter how low blooming is yet too high for the mass of mankind.

None of Spenser's premises is more difficult to the modern reader than this. He seems definitely to reject the formula that simple faith is better than Norman blood. Of base, "dunghill" personages apparently of gentle blood Book VI has several, Briana, Crudor, Turpine, but no case of true virtue in persons of humble origin, unless possibly Melibee. The two other apparent exceptions, Salvage and Pastorella, seem rather to be proofs that courtesy is hereditary, for both are really offspring of gentle parents. Spenser goes out of his way to assure us that Salvage's actions show the results of

> The gentle bloud, how euer it be wrapt
> In sad misfortunes foule deformity. (v, 1)

So with Pastorella. Not long after we meet her we are told that Melibee is not her natural father, but only adopted her (ix, 16). The true rustic is Coridon, whose cowardice and general ineptness is a foil to Calidore's gentility.

77

Yet we cannot take literally this insistence on gentility for virtuous deeds. There is a vast body of comment on the question whether virtue depends on birth, and, as Nelson notes, if Spenser believed that it does, he would be virtually alone. His master Chaucer many times insisted on an innate, not heritable virtue as the true cause of gentle deeds:

> Vyce may be heir to old richesse;
> But ther may no man, as men wel see,
> Bequethe his heir his vertuous noblesse. (*Gentilesse*, 15-17)

Spenser must have been extraordinarily blind not to have noticed the truth of this observation on his own. In fact, once in Book VI Spenser writes in the same vein as Chaucer. When Calepine gives to Matilde the baby of quite unknown parentage, he makes everything depend on nurture:

> And certes it hath oftentimes bene seene,
> That of the like, whose linage was vnknowne,
> More brave and noble knights haue raysed beene. (iv, 36)

As with antiquity, the premise of gentility functions not logically but metaphorically. The order of superiority is not genetic but moral: when a person does a gentle deed he is gentle. The metaphor for the innate virtue that produces virtuous deeds is gentility of birth. Or, as Nelson expresses it, "Manners and deeds are the offspring of the mind; if they are truly gentle, their source must be also." The Salvage Man does a deed only possible to one of gentle birth. Turpine behaves like a poltroon; he is therefore, despite his castle, retainers, and wealth, of the "baser kind," possessed of a "vile dunghill mind."

This leaves Melibee and his virtuous shepherds of Arcady unexplained. To explain them Spenser has counterpoised his premise of gentility with an anti-premise, which in fact is the old pastoral convention. Propositionally stated, this anti-premise would run thus: True virtue resides in simplicity and hence cannot be found in courts, which are rampant with artificiality and self-seeking, but in simple people close to nature like shepherds. The virtue of such people is their innocence, and their innocence is really ignorance. Like the premise of antiquity, this anti-premise of simplicity has interesting historical roots in the conviction found in many societies that the golden age was pastoral. In Genesis this belief is expressed in the slaying of the virtuous shepherd Abel by the farmer Cain, whose descendants found the first city and invent the arts and crafts.

Spenser's thematic development here is somewhat analogous to the thesis-antithesis-synthesis formula of Hegel. The thesis of gentility has its antithesis in simplicity. Calidore, of gentle birth and the product of a court, meets the antithesis of virtuous simplicity in Melibee and his people:

> the happie life
> Which shepherds lead, without debate or bitter strife. (ix, 18)

This life is exemplified in the beauty and grace of Pastorella, and Melibee's eloquence combined with Pastorella's desirability persuade Calidore to abandon the search after "shadows vaine / Of courtly fauour" (x, 2).

Both premise and anti-premise, however, are incomplete and the structure exists only to lead us into the inner meaning of courtesy. The flaw in the complete identification of courtesy with the court is the actuality of the court, the cut-throat strife for advancement which Melibee briefly sketches and which Spenser and many of his readers knew at first hand, and the tendency of the court to substitute artificial courtliness for true courtesy.

On the other hand, the simple life of Arcady is also incomplete. For Melibee it represented a withdrawal—he spent ten years at court. More important, Arcady, the simple life close to nature, is not viable, for it cannot defend itself. With all its faults, the court can do that, for the court is the locus of force, and when Calidore resumes his role of knight he can at least rescue Pastorella. And this is the inner meaning of courtesy: it has to have the advantages of gentility and the training that can be got only in courts, but it must avoid the vices of courtliness and perfect itself in simplicity.

I believe that all of Spenser's premises have similar anti-premises. That of antiquity is modernity, as expressed in the implications of the historical sketches in the first three books, in which the past appears as partly type and partly preparation for the present, for the Elfin line is a type of the Tudors. But the anti-premise of antiquity has little expression in Book VI.

The relationship of Nature and Art exhibits a premise and anti-premise of great pertinence to Book VI. The late C. S. Lewis has shown that the opposition of Nature and Art, of the Garden of Adonis with its rows of growing plants and the Garden of Bliss with its artificial ivy made of gold, is the opposition of fecundity and life to sterility and death. This is one of the dominant themes of the poem, expressed in commentary, image, and narrative.

The premise that fecund Nature creates all good things appears in the proem to Book VI, which returns to the imagery of the Garden of Adonis:

> Reuele to me the sacred noursery
> Of vertue

and the rest of the stanza joins this with a poetic version of the Stoic account of creation:

> Since it at first was by the Gods with paine
> Planted in earth, being deriu'd at furst
> From heauenly seeds of bounty soueraine. (proem, st. 3)

The "seeds" are of course the "rationes seminales" which in the Stoic account of the creative process were implanted in matter. "With paine," I take it, means "with care."

These words are the cue for the entrance of the anti-premise. For, if it is true that fecund Nature produces all good things, it is not true that everything which fecund Nature produces is good. There are flowers, vegetables, and weeds. The Garden of Adonis is a nursery, not a weed patch. A gardener carefully prevents the weeds from choking the desirable plants, but if fecundity were the end in itself—just any kind of vegetation so long as it grew abundantly—then weeds would be preferable to vegetables or flowers.

In fact, many times in the *Faerie Queene* fecund Nature provides symbols of evil in the form of weeds, moss, and hostile animals. In Book II, using the commonplace comparison of the world to a spring whose waters become the more contaminated the further they run from their source, Spenser specifies the form of contamination: "mucking filth" and "uncomley weedes." In Book VI Mount Acidale, though well forested and teeming with birds, has no "wild moss" in its "gentle flud," no "wylde beastes," nor—a fusion with the premise of gentility—does the "ruder clowne / Thereto approach" (x, 7).

A second significant application of both premise and anti-premise of fecundity and growth is the curious double application of the word "ripeness." It appears in Book III to describe the perfection of Amoret in the graces of womanhood: "When she to perfect ripeness grew" (III, vi, 52). The proem to Book VI repeats the formula, this time applied to virtue growing in the "sacred nursery" (st. 3). It is with something of a shock, then, that we next encounter it used to describe the fostering of the Blattant Beast "in Stygian fen / Till he to perfect ripenesse grew" (i, 8).

It is obvious that to Spenser fecundity and the natural processes of growth and maturation may be to good or to evil. This is merely common sense, and there would be no worth in laboring the point if there had not been so much misunderstanding of the relation of Art and Nature.

The anti-premise of malignant fecundity is perhaps less visible than the premise of beneficent fecundity, but it is no less fundamental. The resolution may be stated thus: Nature creates but does not control; Art cannot create, but must control. So true virtue, active as against merely passive, must be a synthesis of Nature and Art. Nature provides the material, and this is the meaning of the premise of gentility—you don't get flowers from weed seeds, but Art must perfect, or the weeds will choke out the flowers. Book VI has several personages equipped by Nature to be courteous but lacking the training: Aladine probably, Calepine certainly, Salvage, Enias, and even Calidore, who cannot accomplish the supreme act of courtesy, the suppression of the Blattant Beast, until he has had experience of simplicity in Arcady.

The *Faerie Queene* has one other structure which one is tempted to call a premise, for it is as pervasive and fundamental as antiquity, gentility, or fecundity. This is the romance form in which it is cast, with the three component elements of chivalry, the quest, and the fairyland setting. Romance, as Spenser uses it, is not merely a literary form or genre or a series of literary conventions. In addition to the narrative effects that he manages to achieve by the romance form, it has also thematic implications. Like the three premises it has deep and widespreading roots and many corollaries. The knight is merely the hero in medieval dress. The quest is the oldest narrative motif. Fairyland, as we have seen, is the place where the three worlds meet; it is also a concretion of the timeless world of ideas, and hence the necessary locus for the functioning of the three premises.

Nevertheless, romance is hardly a premise. It does not yield to propositional statement. The best statement I can discover is, "The perfect exemplification of active virtue is a knight on a quest in fairyland." But this, while indicating the metaphorical function, does not amount to a logical statement. Moreover, romance has no acceptable antithesis.

So it is best to note that the romance form has its thematic implications and to proceed to these. The proper place to begin is to ask why Spenser chose the form. If the Letter to Ralegh has any pertinence in it and at least one of the purposes of the poem is to fashion a gentleman, why did not Spenser choose another form, particularly the epic? As the Letter indicates, the great epics supply good models for the fashioning of a gentleman. So why romance?

The most obvious answer is that romance was popular, in all its several forms, in a way that epic was never to be. We have plenty of contemporary testimony that chivalric romance had a large following among the reading public. Perhaps some of the critics, Ascham and Sidney for example, regretted the size of the audience and thought it principally made up of the semi-literate, the uncultured, and even the vicious. But there is also evidence that a cult of Arthurianism flourished among the highly placed courtiers, who had a Table Round and held tournaments. In fact, the Tudors used the Arthurian legend as political propaganda. For Spenser to have chosen Arthurian romance as his tool to fashion a gentleman, it must have been congenial to him. An author may occasionally choose an uncongenial medium, but he is not likely to stick with it for thousands of lines.

The popularity of Arthurian romance as well as its congeniality to Spenser indicates what its nature was. To the Elizabethan Englishman, Arthurian romance was an image of his national past. Its counterparts to the American of the last half of the twentieth century are the Civil War and the Old West. The Old West has also those qualities of nostalgia and that possibility of rearranging historical experience that makes it a valuable refuge from the present, and because the present always contains the past, there is the constant assumption that the image is a sort of standard to measure contemporary actuality. The popularity of Arthurian romance in Spenser's time is an expression of the same drive that leads our contemporaries to buy cutting horses or join muzzle-loading rifle clubs or, in larger numbers, to consume masses of books about the Civil War and endless horse operas on television.

One of the significant marks of such images is that their clarity and power increase as the actuality recedes. Our own experience with the Old West is a foreshortened and speeded up version of what happened to chivalry. Neither ever existed in the form in which it is represented in the image. But the actualities furnished the beginning point for the image: Charlemagne and Wild Bill Hickok both lived; perhaps also Arthur. Chivalric romance is born as a marriage between the actualities of chivalry and Celtic myth; the Old West of fiction is a marriage between actuality and the conventions of chivalric romance. Each of them becomes stronger and clearer as the events it represents recede further into the past. The distance between event and point of perception makes the image sharper. Since literature cannot digest actuality until it has become image, the best literature of chivalry follows by some centuries the golden age of the actual institution.

This process creates the necessary distance between actuality and literary representation, one sufficiently great to allow perspective, in other words to allow the reader to feel that he is a spectator not a participant, but not too great to inhibit a measure of identification. If the reader identifies so closely that he participates—tries to shoot the villain as audiences sometimes did in the old melodrama—the aesthetic experience vanishes. If, contrariwise the distance is too great, the reader may not wish to cross it. He can just give over reading the work. Doubtless this accounts for some of Spenser's loss of popularity. The image of chivalry is not near enough to our generation; we certainly do not think of it as our own past. A modern Spenser writing for an American audience would certainly use the Old West, which would now and will for a long time in the future establish the correct distance.

Romance absorbed several literary forms and motifs, notably the quest. If one defines literature as something written down (but not strictly in letters) the oldest extant piece of literature in the world is a quest, the *Epic of Gilgamesh*, reduced to writing perhaps as early as 1800 B. C. The quest is not necessarily a metaphor, not, for instance, if it occurs in a story of men seeking uranium, and if the author means and the reader understands that they actually were seeking uranium, which is something worth seeking. Calidore's quest is a metaphor, for the quarry is manifestly not a beast, not even slander, but discourtesy.

This point is worth some laboring, for the issue of Calidore's quest has worried some critics: the Blattant Beast breaks out again and menaces humanity as much now as before Calidore undertook his quest. But to say that the quest is futile is surely to mix metaphor and actuality. The purpose of Calidore's quest is not to end discourtesy for all time. In the total metaphor Calidore must be Everyman as the Beast is every discourtesy. Calidore can muzzle the Beast only for himself, or at most for Gloriana's Court, but not for humanity.

Fairyland is less visible in Book VI than elsewhere. But it would be a great mistake to suppose that Calidore pursues the Blattant Beast outside fairyland. Where else do tigers, bears, and sheep inhabit the same fields? Where else can a civilized lady fleeing from personifications get captured by a band of cannibals? Or a knight catch a fleeing glimpse of the naked Graces atop a mountain?

Fairyland is certainly a sustaining thematic structure of Book VI. Spenser tells us so in the same place where he sets up the premise of antiquity and its anti-premise:

> The waies, through which my weary steps I guyde
> In this delightfull land of Faery
> Are so exceeding spacious and wyde
> And sprinckled with such sweet variety. (Proem, stanza 1)

Despite the relative absence of the marvelous, or at least the supernatural, fairyland is operative throughout the book in the vagueness of time and the fluidity of space, both of which produce the "sweet variety" and delight which Spenser finds as the recompense for his "tedious travell." However unobstrusive it is most of the time, fairyland is as necessary to Book VI as to any other book of the poem.

The thematic entity of romance—which may be defined as the practice of chivalry on a quest in fairyland—has many consequents, of which one of the more pertinent is the relation of prowess to virtue. A superficial glance might report that the virtuous champions are always more puissant than their vicious foes. Redcross knocks over Sans Foy; Calidore dispatches Maleffort and scatters Briana's retainers; Calepine thrusts into the Cannibals and sends them in swarms to hell.

But it is not quite so simple and conventional as "virtue equals strength." Fairyland is peopled not only with puissant champions but also with powerful embodiments of evil, with Orgoglio and Disdain (who are said to be "sib"), who prove sometimes stronger than the champions of virtue, especially when these are caught off-balance. Redcross is disarmed and enervated by the magic stream when he encounters Orgoglio, and the giant conquers him. Timias is holding his own against Disdain, looking for an opening, when his foot slips and Disdain strikes with his iron club. When, somewhat later, Arthur has to rescue both Timias and Enias, he does it more by craft than by strength, dodging and ducking under Disdain's blows, just as he did with Orgoglio and Pyrochles, and just as Redcross did with the Old Dragon. It is not then so much main strength as intelligent tactics that identifies virtue in the *Faerie Queene*. Evil sometimes has the greater power, virtue the greater wit.

III

AFFECT

Sentence, Word, and Stanza

CRITICS WHO HAVE COMMENTED on the effects Spenser creates by his handling of language, apart from narrative or theme, have generally singled out as characteristic a richness of visual imagery, an elaboration of rhetorical figures, a tendency to embellish and decorate often with mythological tags, a purposeful archaism in diction. Probably those who have remarked on the dream-like quality of the *Faerie Queene* have thought of this quality as produced in part by the mechanisms of affect, as distinct from narrative material and pattern.

Though all these characteristics are appropriately predicated of the *Faerie Queene*, especially the last, they do not tell the whole, or even the significant, truth. If uncorrected by being put in perspective, they are particularly deceptive for a study of Book VI. We have already noted that this book contains in smaller concentration the elements specifically characteristic of the romance mode of narrative. It is the same with the accepted characteristics of Spenser's handling of verse. Book VI is basic *Faerie Queene*, in the same way as *Paradise Regained* is basic Milton, lacking as it does much of the color and ornament of *Paradise Lost*. It is what is left over when we subtract exuberance.

Much criticism of the *Faerie Queene* notices the variations and ignores the theme of which they are variations. It is as though one described a printed page in terms of the type face, the rules and ornaments, the line drawings, perhaps even the colored initials or illustrations. Are not these the things that make a printed page? Not quite, for they do not include that which lies between, separates, and defines: the white space, the neutral ground on which all the rest is placed.

An analysis of the affect of Book VI must start with this white space, with the neutral narrative verse which composes a larger bulk of this book than of any other, and which, rather than the more noticed variations, is the basic texture of the work. We can best start by looking at two stanzas, taken almost at random. Serena and Salvage are the actors and the situation is that immediately after Calepine has wandered off and Salvage has by gestures informed Serena of his absence:

> Vpon the ground her selfe she fiercely threw,
>> Regardlesse of her wounds, yet bleeding rife,
>> That with their bloud did all the flore imbrew,
>> As if her breast new launcht with murdrous knife,
>> Would streight dislodge the wretched wearie life.

There she long groueling, and deepe groning lay,
As if her vitall powers were at strife
With stronger death, and feared their decay,
Such were this Ladies pangs and dolorous assay.

Whom when the Saluage saw so sore distrest,
He reared her vp from the bloudie ground,
And sought by all the meanes, that he could best
Her to recure out of that stony swound,
And staunch the bleeding of her dreary wound.
Yet nould she be recomforted for nought,
Ne cease her sorrow and impatient stound,
But day and night did vexe her carefull thought
And euer more and more her owne affliction wrought. (v, 5-6)

The eighteen lines contain nothing that can be called an image. The "as if" clause turns out to be not a simile but a literal comparison: the quantity of blood coming out of her old wounds is equal to what would come out of a new one made by plunging a knife into her breast. Beyond the minimum requirements of verse, meter, rime, and line separation, about the only pattern not expectable in the blandest of prose is the slight alliteration in the fifth line of the first stanza: "wretched wearie life."

The other effects of the passage must be described in negatives: Spenser inserts enough sibilants, dentals, and plosives to prevent any rushing or tumbling effect. The verse does not rumble or roar. On the other hand, there are not enough stops to give the passage a feeling of strain or explosion. Of course, the fact that metric and acoustic effects do not contradict meaning and narrative purpose is testimony to Spenser's control. He chooses to provide almost all the color by the choice of adjectives, most of them coming singly: "murdrous knife," "bloudy ground," "strong swound," "dreary wound." Even so, the majority of the adjectives are definitive rather than descriptive.

Looking at the most technical aspects of the verse, one notices that the rimes are dead center, no slant rimes or assonances to call attention to themselves. To a reader accustomed to the Spenserian stanza, these rimes are so regular as to slip by unnoticed. The only irregularity is the displacement of accents in "There she long groueling and deepe groning lay," and the ambiguous accent in "could best," where sense reading requires "*could* best" and the meter "could *best*."

Naturally, I selected this passage to illustrate the almost complete absence of the commonly noted characteristics of the *Faerie Queene*. The point is, however, that it was easy to find. There are hundreds of such stanzas in Book VI, and together they compose the ground or common style of the book; indeed of the whole *Faerie Queene*. It is a rather bland, effortless, non-aggressive style, self-effacing to allow the reader's main attention to be focused on the narrative line.

Though bland and unself-conscious, this common style is not without its interest. Its syntactic pattern, for instance, is most illuminating. In general, Spenser writes paratactically rather than syntactically. He lays down a statement, which could be complete in itself, then joins to it another statement, then another, and so on, like laying brick, not like putting up structural steel. Thus you could put a period after "Upon the ground her self she fiercely threw," and call it a sentence. But you can add the next line, "Regardless of her wounds yet bleeding rife," and like wise have a complete sentence. Only the fourth line is incomplete and requires you to go on.

Spenser generally mortars his clauses together with loose connectives "and," "but," "for." The result would be condemned as puerile by most teachers of composition. Balanced sentences, periodic constructions, where the beginning protasis demands its completing apodosis, are rare.

It is not that Spenser cannot write the most intricate of rhetorical patterns, with transverse balances and echoes, and all the rest. Earlier in the *Faerie Queene* he had written such patterned passages as

> No tree whose braunches did not brauely spring,
> No braunch, whereon a fine bird did not sit,
> No bird, but did her shrill notes sweetly sing. (II, vi, 13)

And in Book VI one occasionally comes upon antitheses like these:

> So well she washt them, and so well she watcht him. (iii, 10)

and

> Her wauering lust after her wandring sight. (iii, 23)

One imagines that Spenser, living in an age when almost anyone could manage the most elaborate rhetorical figures, found no difficulty in striking off such passages. Most likely, it required a conscious effort to avoid them.

This management of linguistic pattern is essentially colloquial. Spenser is not usually called a colloquial poet, but in the important matter of consistently paratactic construction, with run-on sentences built up of additions he is colloquial, about as much so as Chaucer. There are several reasons why he should be. Spenser is near enough to the advent of printing for him to inherit practices based on the oral rather than the visual consumption of poetry. The romance narrative, from which his practices are derived, incorporates many of the conventions of oral poetry. Suited to the short lyric in verse or the oration in prose, elaborately patterned prose or verse is not a help to narration, but a hindrance. If Spenser had not been bright enough to perceive this for himself, he could have learned it from the fate of *Euphues*, which, despite his popularity, was condemned by the critics Spenser would most have admired.

The danger for the colloquial style is that it can fall into formlessness and flatness. This can easily happen to blank verse or heroic couplets, when written by poetasters satisfied to have ten low words creep in one dull line. But Spenser, of course, is not writing blank verse or heroic couplets, but a highly patterned, intricate stanza with interlaced rimes and a closing hexameter. By the time he came to the passage above he had written approximately three thousand of these stanzas, had thoroughly mastered the stanza form, and knew its possibilities and dangers. The natural tendency of the stanza is elaboration and richness. This possibility is latent and will emerge when Spenser thinks the narrative situation warrants it. In the meantime, he is purposely holding down the possibilities of the stanza.

Perhaps the readiest way to appreciate the special advantages of Spenser's restrained and neutral style is by comparing the passage above with one from another poet, almost contemporary, whose great gifts are opposite those of Spenser. John Donne is only about twenty years Spenser's junior, and his *Progress of the Soul: Metempsychosis* was written in 1601, probably within a decade of the sixth book of the *Faerie Queene*. It is a narrative poem, purporting to tell the progress of a soul from original creation until it animates the body of Luther (or Elizabeth I). Moreover, its stanza is clearly modelled on the Spenserian, even to having a final hexameter. The differences in total affect cannot then be explained by time, genre, or vehicle, and only imperfectly by thematic intention. Here is Donne's account of one of the bodies which the soul animates, that of a sparrow:

> In this worlds youth wise nature did make haste,
> Things ripened sooner and did longer last;
> Already this hot cocke, in bush and tree,
> In field and tent oreflutters his next hen;
> He asks her not, who did so last, nor when,
> Nor if his sister, or his neece shee be;
> Nor doth she pule for his inconstancie
> If in her sight he change, nor doth refuse
> The next that calls; both liberty doth use;
>   Where store is of both kindes, both kindes may freely chuse.

Men, till they tooke laws which made freedome lesse,
Their daughters, and their sisters did ingresse;
Till now unlawfull, therefore ill, 'twas not.
So jolly, that it can move, this soule is,
The body so free of his kindnesses,
That selfe-preserving it hath now forgot,
And slackneth so the soules, and bodies knot,
Which temperence streightens; freely on his she friends
He blood, and spirit, pith, and marrow spends,
    Ill steward of himself, himselfe in three yeares ends. (lines 191-210)

Though the difference in texture between this and the *Faerie Queene* hardly needs laboring, analysis in some detail offers the possible reward of a deeper understanding of the Spenserian method. One quickly notices the number and brevity of Donne's independent clauses, which are not, except for two introduced by *nor*, joined by any connective or transitional element. The clauses vary in length from four to thirty-four words. Variation in pattern is correspondingly extreme. Only one main clause, "he asks her not" has the order of subject-verb-object. One, "men till now . . . did ingress," has subject, long modifying clause, object, and finally verb, a thoroughly syntactic and periodic arrangement.

Of parenthetical, non-restrictive, digressive elements there are few. Inversions, balances, and ellipses are correspondingly numerous, and the whole effect is one of studied periodic structure. The subject-object-verb order, with the objects formed into two pairs, appears in "he blood and spirit, pith and marrow spends;" inversion in "So jolly that it can move / This soule is;" transverse balance with ellipsis of the second element and inversion of the first in "So jolly this soule is / The body so free." These are artful, rhetorical, syntactic structures. Surely the critics who have spoken of Donne's colloquialism have either not been thinking of such passages, or they have misapprehended the nature of the colloquial.

But that is not the question, whether Donne or Spenser is the more colloquial, or whether the special quality of the diction of the *Faerie Queene* is its colloquialism or something else. What we need to get at is the affects and effects of each style. That of Donne is staccato; it is like the seriatim explosion of a string of fire crackers. Though the individual clause is tightly constructed, the clauses are discreet units, with spaces between them. On the other hand, the passage from the *Faerie Queene* is flowing. The discreetness of the elements is not apparent, each seems to melt into the next. Where Donne's statements, because of their individual integrity, call attention to themselves; Spenser's do not. Where Donne is insistent, Spenser is quiet; where Donne is intense, Spenser is diffuse.

Donne's intensity and insistence have merit, but not for narrative. In fact, Donne is not writing narrative. All the narrative in the twenty lines can be reduced to the simple statement that the cock loved promiscuously for three years and then died. The rest is editorializing. This is really what Donne is interested in. The story exists as a frame for Donne to hang an expression of his philosophical libertinism on. This is perhaps to say that theme dominates narrative; and that has been thought to be the characteristic practice of Spenser also, but at least Donne's practice is more explicit than Spenser's. Theme is not so insistent as to inhibit narrative for Spenser; it is for Donne. The *Progress of the Soul* never really gets off the ground as a story, and after 520 lines it falls never to rise again. Nor did Donne ever return to narrative verse, which was obviously not his forte.

Contrariwise, narrative is Spenser's great achievement, over thirty thousand lines of it, terminated by death not by exhaustion. The other merits of the *Faerie Queene* depend on its success as a narrative, and this in turn depends on the quiet, neutral, rhetorically thin style. This style in fact probably covers up a good many defects in thematic realization, even in narrative execution, of the sort illustrated by the Hermit's cure of Serena and Timias, which leaves the reader dangling between metaphor and literal statement. Recent critics who have multiplied examples of this sort of thing have probably been nit picking, but there are enough. That they do not interfere seriously with the reading is mainly due to the continuous parataxis of the style, which carries the reader ever forward so smoothly that he does not notice the motion and therefore does not stop the progress to detect the blemishes.

One point in which Spenser might well be the exotic and Donne the conventional is diction. Ever since Ben Jonson wrote that "Spenser in affecting the ancients writ no language," the archaism of his diction has been an accepted critical dictum. It is not easy for a twentieth century scholar or critic to determine just what was archaic in the late sixteenth century; archaism is largely a matter of contemporary taste and opinion. Every generation of writers is likely to regard its elders as old fashioned, and Jonson's charge may well be that in part. His statement does not positively say, as it has been understood to say, that Spenser's diction is archaic, but apparently that it is neither modern nor ancient. And Jonson's standard is probably not based on actual practice but on some more or less arbitrary rule, so that modern critics need take his opinion no more seriously than they have taken his other judgement that Donne deserved hanging for "not keeping the accent."

Moreover, Spenser could plead two good reasons for at least a flavoring of archaistic diction. One is that a poet follows the best models he can find, which are likely to be in the past and so a little archaic. The best model Spenser can find for English is Chaucer. It would certainly make sense from Spenser's point of view to use Chaucer exactly as the Latins had used Virgil: any word found there is admissible to refined usage. Second, somewhat more convincing to us, is the premise of antiquity. If the events and personages of the *Faerie Queene* belong to antiquity and if their manners and morals were better than those practiced today, it might be supposed that their language would have some superiority also. Or at least, a little of it might be admissible as flavoring.

The question is then whether the amount of archaism is more than that sufficient to establish a feeling of distance. In searching for an answer, I tried the experiment of listing all the apparent archaisms in one canto (the seventh) of Book VI and then looking them up in the *Oxford English Dictionary*, the most comprehensive record of usage available to me, to see whether they were in actual usage in Spenser's age. The list of suspected archaisms was rather small, thirty-seven for the whole canto of fifty verses, or 450 lines, considerably less than one a line. The thirty-seven samples were almost evenly divided between archaic words (*mow, yirk*) and archaic forms of words still in common usage (*brake* and *ensample*).

The results of the check were illuminating. Many of the words had enough citations to attest currency in the late sixteenth century. Other authors used them, sometimes slightly before Spenser, and never apparently in imitation of Spenser's. *Mow, scath, shent,* and *wight,* for instance appear in Shakespeare; *yirk, souse* ("strike"), *spright, carl, bannerall* (usually spelled banneroll), *darrein* (in both meanings: "last," and "to be put out of a religious house"), *stound,* and *inly* all appear to be common enough apart from Spenser's practice. *Aread* ("advise"), *bewray, battailous* appear in Milton, who may have derived them from Spenser, but also in other authors, both before and after Spenser.

Among archaic forms *brake* for *broke, drave* for *drove,* and *ensample* appear in the Authorized Version of 1611, and *nould* from *ne would,* "would not," *swound, drad, mought, vilde, weet* for "wit" are all relatively common. The *Oxford English Dictionary* notes that Spenser's use of *lore* to mean "forsake" or "desert" is incorrect. The same thing might be said of his use of *gan,* which he invariably regards as a clipped form of *began.* Spenser's use of *mote* is labelled "archaistic." *Stour* is described as "used by Spenser and his imitators for a time of turmoil and stress." *Quooke* for *quaked* and *strook* for *struck* are noted only as northern forms. For *tho* ("then") the *Dictionary* gives no citations between 1546 and Spenser, and few for *yearn* ("earn"). One word, *partance,* is not listed at all, and two, *tireling* (a tired horse or person), and *St. Valentide* seem to have been invented by Spenser; they are neologisms, not archaisms.

The total number of archaisms in this canto is then not above seven in fifty stanzas of 450 lines. This is a rather small proportion, about enough to pepper, but not enough to salt, the whole. If canto vii is typical of the book, and there seems no reason it should not be, archaic diction would not seem to be a prominent feature of Book VI.

The complaints of undergraduates that they can't understand Donne and that they can't remember Spenser are illuminating. What these complaints mean is that Donne's details are so clamorous and so little subordinated to a grand design that one gets no sense of over-all pattern, whereas Spenser's details are so subordinated to the onward progress of the whole that they slip by without registering on the memory. Spenser is fluent—no other word fits. The *Faerie Queene* flows, not like a shallow brook with much noise and many eddies and swirls, but like a broad river, where the mass of water presents a smooth surface which conceals all the cross currents beneath.

One reason for this fluency we have already seen, the colloquialism of the syntax, which is not chopped into discrete units but runs on, with units melting one into another. It would be easy to suppose that the Spenserian stanza is the real producer of this phenomenon, that the interlaced rimes and the final alexandrine somehow affect the syntax and push it towards continuity instead of discreteness. If Spenser had been the only poet to use the stanza we might ignore the fact that Donne's rather similar stanza produces quite opposite effects; but Spenser's own stanza in the hands of such diverse poets as Shenstone, Thompson, Byron, Shelley, Keats accomplishes a diversity of effects. *Childe Harold* and *Adonais* have their merits, but they are not those of the *Faerie Queene*.

The stanza is important, but only as Spenser uses it. One of the first things one notes about the stanza of the *Faerie Queene* is that the author uses it as a balancing mechanism, much as Milton does the blank verse line and paragraph. The stanza naturally composes a unit of perception, which the alexandrine at the end naturally closes. The white space separating stanzas from each other and the numbering of each completes the appearance of unity. But Spenser then writes the stanza so as to neutralize this effect. He breaks or introduces a sort of "dip" or "slack" at least once in each stanza and he runs on from the end of one to the beginning of the next. In other words, his stanzas have both caesura and enjambment.

Both of the stanzas quoted earlier in this section have a period at the end of line five. It is accidental that both have a period; it could be a semicolon or a colon, both of them major stops in Elizabethan punctuation. And the break can vary from the middle of line three to the middle of line six, with the two commonest places at the end of line four and at the end of line five. The great majority of all stanzas, and more in Book VI than in earlier books, will be found to have only one such break and that towards the middle. This is not poverty of invention or laziness of execution. Spenser wants it this way. When he varies by putting two or three breaks in the stanza, it is for a purpose, as we shall see when we analyze two passages of heightened tension and quickened tempo.

The great majority of stanzas will also hitch on to the preceding one as these two do. The device used here is pronoun reference. The first stanza has personal pronouns, *herself, she,* the second a relative pronoun *whom.* The relative pronoun is a little tighter connection than usual. Spenser has an array of devices for enjambing his stanzas, some of them quite subtle. Among the grammatical means are connectives of all sorts, ranging from simple coordinating conjunctions (*and, but, for*) to relative pronouns, to adverbial conjunctions (*when, where*), to transitional words and phrases (*thereto, thus, so, then*). In short, he uses all the verbal devices known to his time for tying together separate units of composition, whether verse or prose.

Other methods of achieving continuity are more germane to or peculiar to stanzaic verse. Often, for instance, we find a word in the alexandrine repeated, sometimes in another form, in the first line of the succeeding stanza:

> And eke all knights has *shamed* with this knightlesse part.

> Yet further hast thou heaped *shame* to *shame.* (vi, 33-34)

The repeated element can be a phrase and the distance can be longer than adjacent lines:

> What be you *wofull Dame,* which thus lament,
> And for what cause declare, so mote ye not repent,

> To whom she thus, What need me Sir to tell,
> That which your selfe haue earst ared so right?
> A *wofull dame* ye haue me termed well. (iv, 27-28)

or, finally, the repetition can become a refrain:

> *All raunged in a ring,* and dauncing in delight.

> *All* they without were *raunged in a ring.* (x, 11-12)

Not only words and phrases but rimes can carry over from one stanza to another. A most sustained example is the first four stanzas of the fourth canto, where all four stanzas have one rime in common. The first stanza ends "And his sad Ladie left in pitifull affright," which is picked up in the a-rime of the next stanza: "Till that by fortune, passing all foresight."

The same pattern is repeated in the c-rime of the third and the a-rime of the fourth stanzas:

> And him auenge of that so villenous despight.

> Yet armes or weapon had he none to fight.

What is done with end-rime can also be done with beginning rime, or alliteration, in either of two patterns. The alliteration of the alexandrine can appear once in the succeeding stanza:

> That made them grow so *h*igh t'all *h*onourable *h*ap.

> The Ladie *h*earkning to his sensefull speech. (iv, 36-37)

or vice versa:

> Both his estate, and loue from skill of any *w*ight

> So *w*ell he *w*oo'd her, and so *w*ell he *w*rought her. (x, 37-38)

Certain other acoustical effects also produce fluency. Although the once common assumption that given sounds produce given effects, regardless of meaning, has been deservedly exploded, it still remains true that reading is basically an oral activity—was more so in Spenser's time than it is in ours—and some combinations of sounds are easier to produce than others. One of the best ways of demonstrating this is to put the first line of the *Faerie Queene*,

> Lo I the man, whose muse whilom did make

alongside the first line of *Paradise Lost*,

> Of Man's first disobedience, and the fruit.

Where Spenser's line is loaded with continuants, *l, m, n, h, w, s* (*z*), with only one *th*, two *d*'s, and a *k* as stops, Milton's line has *f, t, d, b, d, f, th, t*. Either poet can write a fluent, either an explosive line, but here, as usually, Spenser chooses to write a fluent one. Stops, especially plosives, are relatively rare in Spenser, as are also difficult consonantal combinations, of the kind that tend to assimilate, like *n* and *p*.

It can hardly be doubted that the increase in continuants, particularly liquids and nasals, and the suppression of stops, particularly plosives, is a large contributor to the fluency of Spenser's lines. Another is his use of the stanzaic structure, particularly the alexandrine. Being one syllable longer, it is heavier and therefore tends to pull the center of gravity of the stanza forwards towards the end. When this is connected or enjambed with the beginning of the next stanza, the effect is of continuity.

The fluency of Spenser's verse does not mean that it is all motion in one direction, with no countermotion or tension. Many of the statements made above are in contradiction: that the stanza is a unit of perception and that it is broken in the middle and joined at the end; that the alexandrine closes the stanza and that it thrusts the movement forward towards the next; that lines are dominantly end-stopped and that each melts into the next. Both ends of such contradictions are true, and that is the tension. The individual stanza does normally make a unit and the alexandrine does emphasize this isolation, but Spenser compensates by breaking the stanza once or often and by connecting each stanza with the succeeding one with a variety of devices.

Fluency comes because here, as in all the other oppositions, a balance is reached between equally heavy weights. In fact it is the great number of such opposites which are resolved that gives the work its sense of quiet. In the early days of the motion picture it was found that the flicker produced by the constant interruption of light in projection could be reduced, not by reducing the number of interruptions but by multiplying them while shortening each, so that three times as many interruptions, each a third as long, produced an effect of steadiness. Something like this phenomenon accounts for the lack of feeling of tension in the parts of the *Faerie Queene* which contain in fact the greatest number of tensions. An analysis of such a scene, the sacrifice of Serena, presented later, shows how this can be.

The achievement of fluency thus needs not mean the absence of tension which is abundantly evident if one looks closely, but it is doubtful if another quality could exist in the same company with fluency and tension. This is compression. Except possibly in a very few passages of rapid action, Spenser does not exhibit compression. He requires a certain amount of padding to do all the other things he wants to do. Tags frequently fill out a line:

> That well appeares in this discourteous knight,
> The coward Turpine, *whereof now I treat.* (vii, 2)

Sometimes whole lines have little content; they only keep the rime scheme:

97

> The whyles his saluage page, that wont be prest,
> Was wandred in the wood another way,
> *To doe some thing, that seemed to him best.* (vii, 19)

A line can be filled out with non-contributory words:

> A Baylieff errant forth in post *did* passe
> Whom they *by name there* Portamore *did* call. (vi, 35)

Or sometimes there is just general verbosity:

> He by the heeles him hung vpon a tree
> And baffuld so, that all which passed by
> The picture of his punishment might see,
> And by the like ensaumple warned bee. (vii, 27)

It is easy to see that such passages carry a good bit of water. Elizabethans did not need to be told that a man hung up by his heels was baffled, or that the purpose of exemplary punishment is for passers-by to take example. Nor can one say, as with Spenser's archaism or his inversions, that Book VI sees a marked diminution over the earlier books. If anything, the expression in Book VI is less compact than in Book I, because of the smaller amount of rhetorical pattern, balance and the like. Whatever path Spenser was following was not taking him towards compression. His models and preceptors, Chaucer and Ariosto, his colloquialism, in which he follows Chaucer, and the whole medieval practice, perhaps the very nature of romance, certainly the scale of his narrative, prohibit compression. Spenser has paid the price of expansiveness by a loss of popularity in an age when force rather than fluency is desired.

Image and Metaphor

TOGETHER WITH A POVERTY of verbal pattern and decoration would seem to go a sparseness of imagery. Certainly in line after line and stanza after stanza one meets only what appears to be the prosaic literal statement of action. The occasional simile, often of the formal epic sort, and the much rarer metaphor seem more often than not conventional, rather than fresh or striking. This experience properly compliments the plainness of the diction and the simplicity of the syntax. We could say that Book VI is thin in imagery, even compared with other parts of the *Faerie Queene*, but that would be accurate only if we made the proper distinctions.

Book VI is sparser in explicit, small-scale imagery than the rest of the poem, in the same measure and for the same reason that it is plainer in rhetorical pattern. But the fundamental structural metaphors, in which narrative line and thematic purpose fuse, are as abundant and pervasive here as elsewhere, and the book is perhaps richer than others in images of smaller scope that deepen the meaning of episodes and personages, without being essential. It is precisely the abundance of these two kinds of imagery that makes the more explicit and decorative ones less necessary.

In both personage and incident Book VI is as dependent on image for its operation as any other part of the poem. Perhaps, since the book deals with courtesy, it is more necessary than elsewhere that the personages who people it, the terrain through which they move, and the events in which they act be recognized as images of the existent world. The thematic validity of the book depends on this recognition. Unless we recognize the actual referent of the Priscilla and Aladine story, unless we identify Turpine with a kind of discourtesy we see daily, the treatment of courtesy in Book VI does not operate. The images must lend perspective by establishing distance, but they must not obscure the meaning.

To give some order to a discussion of imagery, it is useful to distinguish at least three sorts of image. One, the large-scale structural image with ideological content, which functions like a premise in logical discourse, I have called a "premise" and regarded as primarily a thematic mechanism. Besides the premise, one can distinguish at least two other sorts of image. One is repeated or continuous so as to compose a sort of fabric, though it lacks the thematic content of the premise. The other is the simple metaphor or simile, not developed or linked with variations or opposites of itself and used incidentally for description or illustration.

A prime example of the weaving of images into a fabric is the use of

99

light and dark. Light identifies the virtuous, dark the vicious. Hence light glimmering in the dark is virtue persecuted by vice. The Cannibals sacrifice Serena at night, but Serena is identified by images of light. Like many of Spenser's agents of evil, Despair and Mammon, for example, the Brigands live in dark caves where

> darknesse dred and daily night did houer
> Through all the inner parts, wherein they dwelt. (x, 42)

The oxymoron, as Spenser would probably have called it, of "daily night" sets the cue for the imagery of Pastorella's captivity. She has already been described in imagery of light:

> That all the rest like lesser lamps did dim. (ix, 9)

and so throughout the account of her captivity we have images of light obscured or fading. She appears to the Captain

> Like the faire Morning clad in misty fog. (xi, 3)

And when after the fight among the Brigands the survivors find Pastorella wounded in the arms of the dead captain, Spenser takes a whole stanza to elaborate the light versus dark imagery:

> Like a sweet Angell twixt two clouds vphild:
> Her louely light was dimmed and decayd,
> With cloud of death vpon her eyes displayd;
> Yet did the cloud make euen that dimmed light
> Seeme more louely in that darknesse layd,
> And twixt the twinckling of her eye-lids bright,
> To sparke out litle beames, like starres in foggie night. (xi, 21)

The parallel account of the sacrifice of Serena has partly the same pattern of light and dark, but with two differences to differentiate the two pieces. Where the light of Pastorella is dimmed and clouded, that of Serena is interrupted:

> by th'vncertaine glims of starry night,
> And by the twinkling of their sacred fire,
> He mote perceiue a litle dawning sight. (viii, 48)

And, in addition, Spenser adds sound to the description, the shrilling of bagpipes and horns, the confused clamor of the Cannibals, and the shrieking and wailing of Serena. Thus can commonplace imagery be varied and individualized.

Spenser's occupation with birth and growth as a manifestation and metaphor of love is well known. As fecund Nature it becomes a premise, but it also manifests itself in a great many images, some of them of the linked and continuous, some incidental, based on plants or animals. The emphasis on trees and birds in the description of Mount Acidale tells us that we are approaching a holy place, where beneficent Nature rules.

The majority of the plant images in Book VI are, however, of flowers. Courtesy itself is a flower that grows on a lowly stalk, but still spreads bravely abroad (Proem, 4). Sir Bellamoure, Pastorella's father was "in his youthe's freshest flowre" a lusty knight. Pastorella's love for Calidore is expressed by seeds germinating; Calidore's conduct

> in her mynde the seeds
> Of perfect loue did sow, that last forth brought
> The fruite of ioy and blisse. (ix, 45)

When Calepine wants to commend the babe of unknown origin he has rescued from the bear, he suggests that such foundlings are like volunteer plants, whose seed is sown not by men but by gods:

> those braue imps were sowen
> Here by the Gods, and fed with heauenly sap. (iv, 36)

Light and growth imagery join in the simile which compares Pastorella shut up in the Brigand's cave to a flower

> that feeles no heate of sunne
> Which may her feeble leaues with comfort glade. (x, 44)

Animals, including birds, appear more often than plants, and with more variety of reference. Though the Salvage Man is compared to a buck for swiftness (iv, 4) and to a "fawning hound" in his devotion to Serena (iv, 11) and Serena herself, when she is discovered by the Cannibals, to a stray sheep (viii, 36), the most notable animal images have to do with combat. The champions are usually noble animals, their adversaries, if equal, are animals of perhaps less nobility but equal strength, or if ignoble, small and sometimes noxious animals, especially insects. Thus expectedly Arthur leaps on Turpine "like a fell Lyon" (vii, 25) and Calidore attacks the Brigands like "a Lion midst a heard of dere" (xi, 49). Elsewhere Calidore missing Melibee and Pastorella who have been carried off by the Brigands is somewhat unexpectedly a sow bear "whose whelps are stolne away, she being otherwhere" (xi, 25).

Most interesting are fights between rather evenly matched enemies.

Timias fighting Disdain prompts one of Spenser's favorite similes, bull baiting:

> Like as a Mastiff, hauing at a bay
> A saluage Bull. . . . (vii, 47)

where the point of the simile is the pitting of the courage of the smaller mastiff (Timias) against the greater strength but weaker wit of the bull (Disdain). In the two-against-one fight of Arthur against the two knights Turpine has employed, the simile is from falconry:

> As when a cast of Faulcons make their flight
> At an Herneshaw. . . . (vii, 9)

Likewise, for a different purpose, the unarmed Calepine's pursuit of the bear is the flight of a hawk freed from the usual bells and jesses (iv, 19).

A somewhat homelier comparison appears in two similes. When Disdain and Scorn tie up the fallen Sir Enias and again when Calidore throws and muzzles the Blattant Beast, the simile is of throwing a steer. Disdain and Scorn are "a sturdy ploughman with his hynde" who throw the "stub-borne steere," hold him down, and bind him with cords to break him to the yoke (viii, 12). Calidore, however, is a butcher who holds down a bullock "till he be thoroughly queld" (xii, 30). This should be sufficient proof that Spenser's figures though conventional, are not interchangeable.

When the contest is unequal, as when a knight is matched with a rabble, the animal is likely to be small, weak, or noxious. We have already noticed that against Calidore the Brigands are a herd of deer. When fighting among themselves that are "a sort of hungry dogs ymet / About some carcase." Calepine is a hero, but in the unequal contest with the mounted Turpine he runs away like a "wild goat." (iii, 49). With his role reversed, Calepine is a falcon and the Cannibals whom he attacks a "flocke of dawes." (viii, 49). The crowds of riff raff which Talus frequently scatters with his flail in Book V are often compared to insects (e.g. V, ii, 53-54; iv, 44). The same image reappears twice in Book VI, both times with Calidore. When he scatters Briana's retainers he is a steer on a hot summer's day sweeping away "with his long tail the brizes" (i, 24). Again, the Brigands swarm about him as flies on

> whottest sommers day
> Do seize vpon some beast, whose flesh is bare,
> That all the place with swarms do ouerlay
> And with their litle strings right felly fare. (xi, 48)

Another image carried over from other parts of the *Faerie Queene* is the ship. Apparently Spenser's crossings of the Irish Sea had made a lasting impression on him, for the course of a ship, especially one in difficulty, is among the most frequent of his images, for someone in distress, or for the progress of the story or of the hero.* In Book II, for instance, Guyon caught in the middle of the fight between Huddibras and Sans Loy is like "a tall ship tossed in troublous seas" meeting "two contrary billows" and making way by riding "both their backs" (II, ii, 24). The most famous use of the ship simile for the progress of the narrative is in Book I, where the last canto begins with the mariner-poet sighting his haven (I, xii, 1) and ends with a command to strike sails and rest a while in port to put off passengers and refit for the longer voyage still remaining (I, xii, 42).

Book VI uses ship similes for both these purposes. Calepine in unequal combat with Turpine is compared to "a ship with dreadfull storm long lost" with masts and tackle gone "now farre from harbour likely to be lost." But the ship is rescued by a fisher bark, the Salvage Man who appears to drive Turpine off (iv, 1). In his weariness after the fruitless pursuit of the Blattant Beast, Calidore sees himself as a tempest shaken ship. When he comes to Arcady he notes that the Shepherds there are free "from all the tempests of these wordly seas" (ix, 19). Later he asks Melibee for leave "to rest my barcke, which hath been beaten late," (ix, 31) and still later the life of a courtier, which Calidore has abandoned, is embodied in a nautical metaphor:

> fed with light report
> Of euery blaste, and sayling alwaies on the port. (x, 2)

And at the beginning of the last canto of Book VI, Spenser combines the fortunes of Calidore and the progress of the narrative into a simile rather like the one he had used for Guyon:

> Like as a ship, that through the Ocean wyde
> Directs her course vnto one certaine cost,
> Is met of many a counter winde and tyde,
> With which her winged speed is let and crost,
> And she her selfe in stormie surges tost;
> Yet making many a borde, and many a bay,
> Still winneth way, ne hath her compasse lost. (xii, 1)

This is only a variation of one of the great structural metaphors of the whole *Faerie Queene*, time rendered as space, theme and narrative both

* Ships are also frequent in the emblem books.

translated into linear movement. Spenser begins the book with two uses of this metaphor, based on land rather than water travel. In the proem he speaks of

> The waies, through which my wearie steps I guyde
> In this delightfull land of Faery,

which are so "spacious and wide" and "sprinkled with such sweet variety" that the "*travel*," i.e., the labor of composition, loses its tedium (st. 1). And a little later Calidore takes over Artegall's mission "to tread an endlesse trace, withouten guyde" (i, 6).

These are all conventional images and conventionally used. Variety and individuality they have, for instance in the different application of the ship simile to Guyon and to Calidore (or Spenser), but none of the shock characteristic of Donne's flea or his compass. A few of Spenser's images seem to defy the laws of decorum. Calidore behaving in his grief like a sow bear whose cubs have been stolen is not quite a proper picture of the champion of courtesy, either by Scaliger's standards of decorum or by ours. The commercial figures we get when Mirabella, the tables now turned, "is repayed with interest againe" (viii, 21), or Disdain having dealt Enias one stroke,

> with the second stroke, thought certainely
> To haue supplyde the first, and paide the vsury (viii, 9)

may appeal to some tastes as inappropriate, but neither is shocking.

Spenser, however, has his own variety of the shocker. It is the ambiguous, the ambivalent, the ironic image. We have already seen him using not merely the same image but the same formula for Amoret and the Blattant Beast. There is enough of that sort of thing to indicate that it was purposeful, not accidental.

For instance, heat, flame, fire appear often with reference to immoderate passion, usually anger or love. Pyrochles' entrance into the action of Book II is attended by a chain of such images (II, iv, v), as is the affair between Paridell and Hellenore (III, ix), where the eloping lovers literally set Malbecco's castle on fire. But the same imagery serves to express Calidore's admiration of the stripling Tristram's courage:

> thy kindled courage set on fire
> And flame forth honour in thy noble breast. (ii, 37)

and Calidore's honest love for Pastorella:

When to the field she went, he with her went;
So for to quench his fire, he did it more augment. (ix, 34)

So, too, with gardens. Usually an image of productive love, a garden can be perverted as in the Bower of Bliss, and can be used as a figure of the courtier's life by Melibee, who "in the Princess gardin daily wrought" (ix, 24). Bagpipes when played by the Cannibals at the sacrifice of Serena (viii, 46) are an image of evil—at least there was a long tradition that condemned all wind instruments, and Spenser, remembering Chaucer's Miller and his own experience in Ireland, probably accepted it. But the bagpipe is also the instrument with which Colin Clout pipes to the dancing Graces.

These instances of ambivalent imagery are perhaps more curious than significant. In at least one instance the ambivalence becomes important. The health of the body was the medieval preacher's favorite metaphor for the health of the spirit; disease or wound is sin, and the administration of the sacrament of penance is a physician curing a diseased patient. So the effects of spiritual pride on Redcross becomes a weakness of the body, and the cure of the desperate morbidity he contracts in Orgoglio's dungeon is the medicine of the House of Holiness.

Expectedly, then, the injury of Slander becomes a wound inflicted by the Blattant Beast which becomes infected and refuses to yield to the normal curative process. Both Serena and Timias are suffering from this wound when they meet. Already we have a little difficulty. Redcross' bodily illness was strictly analogous to his spiritual, and both were, each on its own level, caused by his own failures and mistakes. Are Serena's and Timias' wounds the results of their own choices? We can perhaps blame Serena for wandering away from the protection of Calepine and Calidore, but we find nothing wrong in Timias' conduct. He is the victim of enemies, who have set the Blattant Beast in his way, and of chance, whereby his foot slips when he is winning over the Beast. The analogy has some faults in it.

These widen when we pursue the course of the cure. If the result of slander is an infected wound, then the remedy ought to be something that heals an infected wound. We can recognize the existence of psychosomatic illness, even allow that Spenser knew of the entity, but an infected wound is not psychosomatic. Hence the cure ought to be something like the treatment Patience performs on Redcross (I, x, 23-34), a cauterizing of the wound, but the Hermit does nothing of the sort. He admits the ineffectiveness of physical medicine and reads the two victims a long lecture on the avoidance of the occasion and appearance of evil.

The ambivalence which becomes confusion in the image of disease probably reflects an ambivalence in Spenser's own attitude. Either he had not made up his mind about slander or about disease. Or perhaps he has not resolved conflicting traditions. The latter is certainly the explanation for some puzzling metaphors in the account of Calidore's love for Pastorella. A long tradition, enshrined in many a sonnet, saw the onset of love as a wound from Cupid's arrow. Sometimes the arrows are poisoned and the wound becomes infected. We are not surprised, then, to find Calidore's love "feeding on the bayt of his own bane" (ix, 34), but the subsequent development in such phrases as "enuenimd sting," "poysnous point," and "ranckle sore" seems to sort ill with the image of infection-assin.

And what are we to make of Pastorella's "sodaine sickness"? At first we learn that it was feigned to escape the unwanted attentions of the Brigand Captain (xxi, 7). If this is the case, the sickness is not a metaphor or figure, but a literal narrative detail. But presently it is spoken of as real, not feigned: "her sickness was not of the body but the mynde" (st. 8), and when the merchants want to buy her she is described as "decayd and mard," though still beautiful "like a Diamond of rich regard / In doubtfull shadow" (st. 13). Is this uncertainty and apparent change of direction due to haste, or to a real ambivalence in Spenser's own sensibility? Or is it inherent in the thematic situation?

The answer is not simple or single. Partly it is inherent in the material, a reflection of the ambiguity of the human condition. Calidore's love of Pastorella is on one level a dereliction from duty: he should be pursuing the Blattant Beast. Instead, he lingers in Arcady, the lure of pastoralism, which, in the moral equivalence is whatever entices one from the duty of moral perfection. To be enticing, the pastoral world must have some good in it, at least an appearance of good, and Spenser makes his pastoral world alluring, just as he had done with the Bower of Bliss. Obviously, Spenser himself is attracted by the spiritual and moral retreat symbolized in the pastoral life. After all, he is the greatest pastoral poet in English.

But just as obviously Spenser has seen through pastoralism and has repudiated it. Perhaps his experience in Ireland, where the true nature of "simple folk" was painfully apparent; perhaps his own native hardheadedness told him that pastoralism is really an avoidance of the issue and a slinking from the good fight. Pastorella, who should embody the essence of pastoralism, is somewhat ambivalent, too. She is not really a shepherdess, as her name indicates, but the daughter of a knight. Hence Calidore's love for Pastorella is doubly ambiguous, a love placed in an apparently wrong object, which however, because it is not what it seems, is actually the right object. Serena, too, has her doubleness of being; the name seems ironic, and neither she nor Timias are quite innocent victims of slander. They have apparently cooperated in producing their own hurt.

Perhaps this is over sophisticated. A simpler way to state the case is merely to say that both the simple life and slander are in nature ambivalent and that Spenser sees this ambivalence and reflects it unconsciously in the mixed imagery in which he embodies his treatment of these themes.

Such an attitude is not characteristic of Spenser. If it were he might be more popular in an age which admires unresolved tensions in its art and rewards poets who make us "walk an intellectual or emotional tight rope between two worlds." The characteristic Spenser prefers a bland, untense story which flows effortlessly along, adorned by occasional images, mostly of a quite conventional sort, but never too many. Then occasionally, at almost predictable intervals, the metaphors multiply and the imagery thickens, description dominates narration, and we have a "set piece" or a "purple passage." Such are the enclosed narrative of Mirabella, the capture and rescue of Serena, the epiphany on Mt. Acidale, the capture and rescue of Pastorella.

The beginning of the Mirabella episode is signalled by a sudden increase in rhetorical patterning. In four stanzas (vii, 28-31) the word love occurs seven times, and two alexandrines exhibit purposeful repetition:

> And noblest she, that serued is of noblest knight (st. 29)
> What could the Gods *doe more*, but *doe* it *more* aright. (st. 31)

Other patterns include: simple alliteration on accented syllables;

> Or who did *w*ayle or *w*atch the *w*earie night
> *L*et them that *l*ist their *l*ucklesse *l*ot dep*l*ore (st. 30)

alliteration with a sliding assonance;

> And so would *e*ver l*i*ve and l*o*ve her owne delight (st. 30)

parallelism with alliteration;

> *S*tubborne *s*tiffnesse and *h*ard *h*art (st. 31)

parallelism with the second element reversed;

> meane parentage and kindred base. (st. 28)

This sudden increase in rhetorical patterning, which would mean little if the author were Donne, and somewhat less if it came earlier in Spenser's work, is extremely significant here. It is the cue to the reader to slow up and prepare to read more closely. The increase in pattern precedes an increase in metaphor, that is explicit, relatively small-scope metaphor. In fact the account of Mirabella's crime and punishment is but a development of one or at most two metaphors. Her discourtesy is cruelty to her suitors. This Spenser translates into two closely associated figures: Mirabella's suitors are feudal retainers of Cupid, and hence her mistreatment of them is a crime against Cupid, and her punishment becomes a trial and sentence in his court.

As Spenser develops the metaphor, Lord Cupid holding his court on St. Valentine's Day ("Valentide") discovers when the rolls are read that many of his vassals are absent. Taking his blindfold off, Cupid finds that they are missing, imprisoned, exiled, or dead. A grand jury is impaneled and finds that Mirabella is responsible. Cupid then commands a writ of "capias" to be issued, which a bailiff named "Portamore" serves on Mirabella, attaches her, and hales her before the bar. She stands mute until a judgment is pronounced, which, though it is not specified, is probably death. Mirabella then asks for mercy, whereupon Cupid mitigates the unspecified sentence to a penance of wandering in the company of Disdain and Scorn until she has saved as many souls as formerly she lost.

So far this has been consistently one metaphor, that of a feudal lord with the combination of legal powers which such lords possessed. At this point the metaphor changes somewhat. Civil courts do not commonly assign penances. Scholars have suggested that the scene derives from the "court of love," or that Mirabella's punishment is a use of the medieval motif of the "purgatory of dames." More simply, Spenser is probably continuing the metaphor of a court, but making it ecclesiastical rather than civil. Sentences of pilgrimage, which is essentially what Mirabella's wandering is, or of some sort of task involving both physical hardship and humiliation, are common enough from ecclesiastical courts, which, be it remembered, had in the middle ages nearly exclusive jurisdiction over marriage and therefore the legal aspects of love and sex. And of course, the literary convention of the court of love underlies the whole Mirabella episode.

In some ways Mirabella is an excursus. An enclosed episode of brief duration, it bears on the theme of Book VI, since it exemplifies the application of courtesy to love, but it lies rather outside the mode of the book, for instance, in having personifications, Disdain and Scorn. Though not a digression, it is not an integral part of the thematic line, as is, for instance, the capture and rescue of Serena.

The capture of Serena by the Cannibals follows her rapid flight, when Disdain and Scorn throw and bind Timias. Serena's flight is told in rather bland though rapid-paced narrative. As soon as she stops her headlong flight, an increase in pattern and image again foretells a change in texture. When Serena goes to sleep it is with an allusion to Morpheus (viii, 34), followed soon by a personification: "False Fortune did her safety betray." Then comes the information that in the "wyld deserts" where she now is dwells a "saluage nation" who neither plow nor herd nor trade, but nightly raid their neighbors "And serue their owne necessities with others need."

The word "nightly" sets up one of the two contrapuntal images of the scene, darkness, black, and night for the Cannibals and their deed, light, whiteness for Serena. The Cannibals see the face of the sleeping Serena "like yuory shining." As the Cannibals strip her we have this whiteness and shininess driven home: "golden locks, and snowy breasts" (viii, 40), and later

> Her yuorie necke, her alabaster brest . . .
> Her tender sides, her bellie white and clere. (st. 42)

As the Cannibals take Serena to the sacrificial altar, dusk is falling. The skies are first brazen (st. 40), then black:

> and now the Euentyde
> His brode black wings had through the heauens wyde
> By this dispred. (st. 44)

Night is not only a black bird, it is also surely a bird of prey, a raven or a vulture. Visually, the rest of the scene is developed as sparks of light amidst a surrounding darkness. Calepine perceives what is going on by the "uncertain glims of starry night" and by the "twinkling of their sacred fire."

But this is only one strand of the total fabric. Weaving through the fabric is also the altar image. The actual altar made of turves which the Cannibals built is anticipated by the comparison of Serena's body to an altar:

> Her tender sides, her bellie white and clere,
> Which like an Altar did it selfe vprere
> To offer sacrifice diuine thereon. (st. 42)

The comparison of the pelvis to an altar seems to have a history, hinted at in the name of one of the pelvic bones, the *os sacrum*. Donne uses a similar figure in the "Epithalamion Made at Loncolnes Inne," where the bride lies

> Like an appointed lamb, when tenderly
> The priest comes on his knees t'embowell her. (11. 89-90)

The priest's knife, emphasized by Spenser, also must have a phallic significance.

The altar soon dissolves into another architectural image:

> Her goodly thighes, whose glorie did appeare
> Like a triumphall Arch, and thereupon
> The spoiles of Princes hang'd, which were in battel won. (st. 42)

The quietness of the syntax, the absence of rhetorical adornment may deceive the cursory reader to the explosive power really contained in this series of images. For one thing, Spenser is building up with the images another motif which will become dominant in the next stanza: the sensual attraction of the naked Serena that nearly pulls the Cannibals from their religious duty. Their lust almost breaks through, and the priest has to rebuke them "not to pollute so sacred threasure." The omniscient author ends the stanza with a brief moralization: "Religion held euen theeues in measure."

The religion which composes one side of this religion-versus-lust tension is of course the vilest form of cruelty and superstition: after dedication to their god, the Cannibals will eat Serena. Through the reader's mind flits the question whether, under the circumstances, lust is not more honest than religion. The irony is underlined for anyone who recognizes the source which Spenser is parodying in his image of the arch. Many sixteenth-century readers would have remembered the source passage in the Song of Songs, 4:4: "Thy neck is as the tower of David built for defence: a thousand shields hang therein, and all the targets of the strong men,"* perhaps also other architectural imagery for the body of the beloved elsewhere in the same book: "If she be a wall, we will build upon her a silver palace" (8:9) and "I am a wall and my breasts are as towers" (8:10).

The capture of Serena illustrates still another method by which Spenser can develop excitement and tension, with less effort than Donne, for example, would require. In the passage from the *Progresse of the Soule* we noted how short were the syntactic units in comparison with Spenser's, where a complete syntactic unit, an independent clause, normally requires half a stanza, four or five lines. Spenser can heighten the excitement by the simple device of shortening the unit. In the twelve stanzas which compose the sacrifice and rescue of Serena (st. 40-51) we note exactly this. The first of the series of stanzas (40) has a break in the middle of the seventh line; the second (41) has breaks within the first line, after the third, the fourth, and the seventh; the following two (42-43) have two breaks each, at the ends of the third and sixth lines, and at

---

* I cite the Geneva version, the one most likely known to Spenser.

the end of the third and middle of the ninth, respectively. Two units of less than a line each, "but all boots not" (41), and "religion held even theeues in measure" (43), give a slightly staccato effect.

The last arrangement, with the epigrammatic, hypermetrical "Religion held euen theeues in measure," is particularly effective. The next stanza (44) has two breaks, mid-fourth and end of the seventh, then at the end of the third and seventh; then a one line unit in the middle of the stanza, line five, with breaks before and after. Stanza 47, which briefly recounts Calepine's search for Serena, goes back to the one-break pattern, obviously because it marks a pause for a change of narrative direction, but three of the remaining four stanzas have two breaks each.

Besides the visual imagery there is also auditory. As images of light and dark play against each other, so do effects of quiet and noise. When Serena first wakes to find the Cannibals clustered round her, her heart quakes, her face blanches and "aloud she cries." The following four stanzas occupied with the visual description of the naked Serena and the building of the altar, have no mention of sound, then the priest as he approaches with upraised knife mutters a charm and the sound resumes. The Cannibals shout, the bagpipes and horns begin to shrill. Serena's wailing is drowned out by the din:

> The whiles she wayled, the more they did reioyce.

Finally, imagery also serves a narrative purpose: it often foreshadows and plants for coming events. For instance, there is the iteration of "naked." First it describes Serena (st. 41); next it is the priest's arm that is naked (st. 45), and finally Calepine sees

> one with a naked knife
> Readie to launch her brest, and let out loued life.

Or the images may sew together the narrative, serving the same function as connectives, anticipating and summarizing phrases, and cross references in ordinary writing. The image of insects, one of Spenser's favorites for describing a group of inferiors, appears when Serena awakes to see the Cannibals surrounding her: "round about her flocke, like many flies." It then reappears when Calepine sends "swarmes of damned soules to hell." Likewise with sacrifice. The Cannibals would literally sacrifice Serena; metaphorically, it is Calepine who sacrifices the priest "to th'infernall feendes."

The capture and rescue of Serena is texturally the densest passage in Book VI. Some others approach it, the Mirabella episode, as we have seen, the dancing maidens on Mount Acidale, the fight of the Brigands over

Pastorella. In all of these one observes the same approach, a thickening of rhetorical pattern and imagery, usually concurrent with a shortening of the syntactic unit. These phenomena are also characteristic of the set pieces in which the earlier books abound, the House of Holiness and the House of Pride in Book I, and even Mercilla's Court in Book V. But there is one notable difference between the House of Pride and Serena's capture. The former is dominantly descriptive. Narrative freezes for a while as the parade of the Seven Deadlies is described. Nothing stops for Serena; rather the narrative speeds up. Book VI has no set pieces on the earlier model; Spenser has absorbed the set piece into the narrative, making of the high points of action equivalents of the earlier set piece.

Comedy

WHEN MILTON LABELLED Spenser "our sage and serious poet" and preferred him as a teacher to Scotus or Aquinas, he insured that generations of critics would fail to perceive Spenser's undoubted comic talents. Though Milton can hardly be held responsible, civilization was entering a period when serious purpose and humor would be regarded as incompatible. In volume after volume of criticism you will look in vain for any recognition of Spenser's achievements in the comic. At best, you will find some grudging comment like, "This seems to be one of Spenser's few consciously humorous passages."

Yet in its own way the fabliau of the lustful young Hellenore, the aged and avaricious Malbecco, and the sly seducer Paridell rivals Chaucer's best, and the braggart Bragadocchio deserves a place beside Falstaff. These are perhaps the heights of Spenser's comedy and they come in Books II, III, and IV. Book VI has nothing quite so sustained as these nor as obvious as the story of the Squire of Dames, also in Book III, who in three years time found only three women proof against his wooing, and of these one was a courtesan whose price he would not pay and another a nun who was afraid he would not keep her confidence.

The similarity of the Squire of Dames to such passages as the host's story in canto xxviii of *Orlando Furioso* ought to remind us that the model Spenser adopted for the *Faerie Queene* was the romance as practiced by the Italians Boiardo, Ariosto, and Tasso, which is noted by all critics for its irony, raillery, and urbane cynicism. It would be strange if, while borrowing so much of narrative organization, incident, and character, Spenser had permitted none of the tone or mood to be carried along. That Spenser's purpose is more serious than that of Boiardo and Ariosto, if perhaps not of Tasso, admits no doubt, but that he does not completely abandon the levity of the great Italians can be demonstrated by two parallels.

Boiardo affords the first. In a struggle with a giant, Orlando has become enmeshed in a magic net of iron which he cannot break. The place is completely desert, and Orlando is likely to perish of hunger and thirst. A monk passes by. No good Samaritan, he is concerned more with his own safety than with rescuing Orlando. Still he must make some contribution; so he preaches a long sermon on the sufferings of the martyrs, who was crucified, who flayed alive. All suffered greater torments than Orlando, who, even though he must die, should thank God in heaven. Desperate as his situation is, Orlando does not lose his poise: he responds humbly with, "Thanked be God, but not for this."[*]

The absurdity of the situation, the wry comment delivered by understatement find a parallel in the passage in Book VI which even the editors of the Variorum label "one of Spenser's few consciously humorous passages." On a walk through the countryside Calepine has encountered a bear with a babe in his mouth. The bear has dropped the babe to meet Calepine's attack. Calepine, lacking weapons, picks up a stone and thrusts it into the bear's open mouth. The comment, supplied by the author in the name of the bear, is that the beast is "nigh choked,"

> Being vnable to digest that bone;
> Ne could it vpward come, nor downward passe. (iv, 21)

The second parallel is to a passage in Ariosto. It starts off as a tall tale. Ambushed, Orlando has to fight with a troop of knights. He is so furious and the danger is so great that he rides at them piercing one after the other with his lance until he has skewered six of them. The lance is full, so the seventh, after being pierced, falls off. Accustomed as we have become to superhuman feats by the heroes of romance, we are a bit slow in waking up to the fact that we have been had. Ariosto first signals the game he is playing by a comparison of the knights to dough. The more sophisticated readers will detect the deception at this point; the less perceptive must wait for the simile which caps the piece. Orlando's action is compared to a skillful spearman gigging frogs and not stopping to remove them until the whole shaft is filled (*Orlando Furioso*, ix, 68-69).

Spenser uses precisely this technique in Calidore's charge into Briana's castle, with an even more artful build-up than Ariosto's. The champion of courtesy interrupts Briana's seneschal, Maleffort, who is preparing to cut off a maiden's hair. Maleffort turns on Calidore with a scornful reference to Calidore's lack of beard. Then follows a deceptively commonplace account of the fight with such details as "hideous strokes" and "importune might." We even have an epic simile, one of Spenser's usual methods of highlighting an important fight, here comparing Calidore's fury with a mill stream. Maleffort flees, Calidore catches up with him and splits his skull just at the castle gate, so that the corpse blocks the gate and the retainers cannot close it against Calidore. The retainers flock about Calidore, and we are all set up for a grand melee. But we get nothing of the sort. Just as Ariosto did, Spenser lets us know that we have been had by giving us instead of blood and blows a simile:

[*] "Rispose Orlando, con parlar modesto
Ringraziato sia lui, ma non di questo." (*Orlando Innamorato*, I, vi, 20)

But he [Calidore] them all from him full lightly swept,
As doth a Steare, in heat of sommers day,
With his long taile the bryzes brush away. (i, 24)

This view of the hind end of a steer is not the only element of incongruity in the scene. The whole episode of Briana's castle is delivered in the comic spirit. Briana's task, the weaving of a mantle for her lover from the hair of knights and ladies is fantastic, perfectly suited to the lady's complete lack of self-perception. Her denunciation of Calidore, for the same sort of invasion of the rights of others as she has been committing, as well as the character of Crudor, the lover for whom she is going to all the trouble, are all, when viewed objectively, comic.

If we seek reasons why Spenser's comedy has gone mostly undetected, whereas that of his masters, Chaucer and the Italians, is universally recognized, two obvious ones strike us. The first is the dichotomy, apparently peculiar to a bourgeois-protestant society, which rejects the possibility of combining moral or ethical purpose with comic formulation. Recent critics have shown that Chaucer's *Nun's Priest's Tale*, for instance, is a homily on pride, quite seriously intended. The obviously burlesque tone of the piece has blinded us to the serious moral it enforces. Precisely the same thing has happened, only reversed, to Spenser. Because the Hellenore-Malbecco-Paridell episode is so apposite an illustration of certain perverse types of love, critics have missed the fabliau quality of the tale, as well as the fact that it is a burlesque of the classical Helen-Menelaus-Paris story.

That single-minded critics have seized on Spenser's moral or ethical import instead of his comic method of expression is probably due to elements of Spenser's style which we have noticed: its neutrality and self-effacement combined with fluency and speed. Spenser's humor is almost all dead-pan. The clues and signals which indicate the comic are of the most unobtrusive sort, so that the unsubtle can easily miss them. If one is following, in addition to a complicated story line, two separate supposed lines of "allegory," a moral and a political, it is no wonder that he misses something which he never expected to find anyway.

One cue that the searcher for moral meaning might follow is the moral judgment which the author passes on an incident or a personage. It is a critical commonplace that comedy, except for some kinds of satire, lies outside the moral conventions of a society. If the audience regarded Falstaff as a highwayman, there would be no fun in the play. Spenser follows precisely this practice in his treatment of Hellenore and of Braggadocchio. Nowhere does he pass judgment on the lustful wench. If anyone suffers, it is the wronged husband who loses both property and wife. Hellenore gets what she wants, complete physical satisfaction, and

Paridell, the seducer, goes scot free. So with Braggadocchio. He almost gets away with it, and his final come-uppance is only to be shown up for what he is. The villain is not punished; the clown is unmasked.

To a considerable extent this applies to the chief comic episodes of Book VI. Maleffort, Briana's seneschal, loses his life, but otherwise Briana and Crudor go unpunished. In fact, Briana gets what she wants, the love of Crudor. Everyone must note the difference in the resolutions of this episode and the succeeding one, where the Knight of the Barge is slain by Tristram. Turpine is also handled rather gently. After all the trouble he has caused, including the deaths of "heaps" of his followers slain by Salvage, and the unnamed errant knight Arthur is forced to kill, his final punishment seems rather trivial: he is left hanging by the heels.

Another signal of comic intent is verbal. This can be negative, the absence of moral comment where one would expect it, or positive, as in the simile of the steer sweeping away the flies, which sets the tone of the whole episode. This is one of Spenser's favorite devices, the use of either figurative or literal descriptions which establish a discordance between the apparent and the real significance of an action.

We might call this "verbal humor," and set up "situational humor" as its opposite. This is a useful distinction, if we do not ride it too hard. The *Faerie Queene* is a poem; hence all its humor comes to us in verbal dress, not in action, as in a play. Moreover, much comedy depends on the attitude of the observer, or reader. Being hit in the face with a custard pie is not funny if we identify with the victim. It may be if we take a detached and objective point of view. In a verbal art form the point of view the reader takes depends almost entirely on the author's handling of language. Hence even in the nearest approach to situational humor in the *Faerie Queene*, Spenser is intervening with language between the pure situation and the reader-observer.

How much difference the choice of language can make appears in the incident in Turpine's castle when Turpine and his followers set on Arthur and Salvage. Whether this is serious or funny depends on the attitude of the reader. Since, in the nature of things, the reader must identify with Arthur and Salvage, his attitude then depends on the seriousness of the threat. If Arthur and Salvage really have to fight for their lives, then it is not funny. If, however, they are in no real danger, then the situation can develop as comedy. With a coward like Turpine in command, there can hardly be a serious threat; hence Spenser chooses to develop the situation as comedy. His signal is, as with Calidore at Briana's castle, the simile, a comparison of the fight to bull baiting, in which Arthur is the

> fierce Bull, that being busie bent
> To fight with many foes about him ment,

and Turpine becomes a little cur biting at the Bull's "heeles" from behind (vi, 27). This puts things in their true perspective, frees us from any worry about either protagonist, and allows us to be amused at the cowardice of Turpine.

The manipulation of words to set attitude can take diverse forms. The two examples we have noticed are both similes, but this is not invariable. The effect of incongruity can as well be created by the choice of low words, as when the Blattant Beast's mouth is described as being big enough to contain

> A full good pecke within the vtmost brim
> All set with yron teeth in raunges twaine. (xii, 26)

At first glance this reduction of the fearful Blattant Beast, who is the supreme expression of evil in the book, comparable to the old dragon of Book I, might seem a mistake by Spenser. And it would be, if it were anywhere else but at the end of the book, after the Beast has been bayed. At this point the denigration of the great opponent is quite consonant with Spenser's thematic purpose.

Another form of verbal humor is intentional understatement to produce an effect of bathos. Salvage's rescue of Calepine from Turpine's persecution illustrates this. Armed and horsed, Turpine has chased the unarmed and unhorsed Calepine around like a goat. Then Salvage charges Turpine and the situation turns about; from being pursuer Turpine becomes pursued, and

> Gan cry aloud with horrible affright
> And shrieked out. . . .

This is funny enough, but Spenser caps it with a monstrous understatement:

> a thing vncomely for a knight. (iv, 8)

Or the incongruity can be damnation by faint praise, as in the account which the lady of the Knight of the Barge gives of Priscilla:

> Faire was the Ladie sure, that mote content
> An hart, not carried with too curious eyes. (ii, 16)

In other words, Priscilla is beautiful, if one doesn't look too closely. The real humor of the passage derives, however, from the situation. The speaker is the lady whose lover deserted her for Priscilla. She is quite aware, as her story shows, that Priscilla is entirely innocent of any intent to lure the Knight of the Barge away from his companion, but there is still a residuum of resentment that shows up in the lady's speech.

The comedy here is partly situational. At its vanishing point verbal humor may only be a choice of language to provide a point of view so unexpected or unconventional as to produce the shock of discrepancy that underlies the comic. When Calidore sees Maleffort seizing the golden locks of a maiden he defies the seneschal, and we conventionally interpret his defiance as a deed of nobility. Maleffort puts a different interpretation on the defiance: Calidore is offering to exchange his beard for the maiden's tresses, and it isn't a fair bargain:

> And for this Mayd, whose party thou doest take
> Wilt giue thy beard, though it but little bee?
> Yet shall it not her lockes for raunsome fro me free. (i, 19)

A few stanzas later Maleffort himself is the victim of this sudden shift in point of view. His death is viewed by the author as important principally as preventing the people in the castle from closing the gate:

> The carkasse tumbling downe within the dore,
> Did choke the entrance with a lumpe of sin,
> That it could not be shut, whilest Calidore
> Did enter in. . . . (i, 23)

Another application of an eccentric point of view is the comments of the Cannibals on the sleeping Serena. They regard her solely as something good to eat, appraising her anatomical parts as a butcher would a beef. They debate whether to kill her before she wakes, whether to make one big feast or "many meales." This goes on for four stanzas and into a fifth, with only one adjective, at the very beginning, to indicate that there is anything abnormal in the situation. Beyond the description of cannibalism as "one most accursed order," the passage is all straightfaced and dead-pan. When Serena awakens we get an alternation of points of view, Serena screaming and the Cannibals going about their preparations. The high point of grim humor is reached in the compromse between the priest who wants her sacrificed and the rest of the company who want to eat her: her blood will go to their god, her flesh to the Cannibals.

Also on the borders between the verbal and the situational is the device used several times in the *Faerie Queene* of having the criminal turn accuser. A good sample of this is the tirade which Briana looses on Calidore:

False traytor Knight (sayd she) no Knight at all,
But scorne of armes that hast with guilty hand
Murdred my men and slaine my Seneschall
Now comest thou to rob my house vnmand,
And spoile my selfe, that can not thee withstand? (i, 25)

This is delivered with such vehemence that even Calidore is momentarily taken aback. But of course the discrepancies are apparent on examination. Calidore has not murdered her men, only scattered them. He slew Maleffort, the seneschal, but in the performance of his duty, so to speak, and the imputation of intent to rob the castle and rape Briana is a commentary on Briana's own moral standards.

The very nature of chivalric romance opens up a world of possibilities for situational comedy. After all, a prime comic situation, some would say root of all comedy, is shocking disparity. Popular cartoon series manufacture comedy out of a king sewing on a button or a monk asking his companions what the Latin is for bingo. Like kings and monks, the personages of chivalric romance belong to a superior realm. Put them in the ordinary world and you have the possibility of comedy.

In this sense almost the whole of Book VI is situational comedy, for the theme of the book requires that the situations be rather ordinary ones, for courtesy is a virtue peculiar to this social world which lies between the superior and inferior realms to which romance as well as myth properly belong. Over and over again we recognize behind the mask of romance the actualities of ordinary life. The instant we make such a recognition, for example that the predicament of Priscilla and Aladine is really that of a teen-age couple parked in a lovers' lane and becoming the victims of a "love bandit," that instant we have the possibility of the comic instead of the serious interpretation.

On the other hand, the relative lack of the more obvious forms of magic and wonder which commonly characterize romance makes the disparity somewhat less, if more frequent, than in other parts of the *Faerie Queene*. Whether a particular reader finds an episode uproariously funny (few are that), merely amusing, or not worthy a smile depends on what aspect of the totality he is concentrated on. Take for instance, the episodes of Calepine and the bear. If we have made a series of translations which have reduced chivalry, fairy-land and myth to completely transparent enclosures of familiar social patterns—if we are completely concentrated on theme—there is nothing funny about the incident. The same is true if we are literally following the narrative.

But if we are shifting our gaze from one aspect to another, now aware of Calepine as a knight of romance, a creature far removed from us, now aware of the triviality of what he is doing, taking a stroll, then the disparity begins to function: Sir Launcelot holding a squalling infant.

Almost the whole of Calidore's stay in Arcady has this quality of absurdity. Calidore is a fighting man; when he doffs armor for a shepherd's weeds, he sets up a discrepancy. The episode begins with Calidore behaving like an adolescent. Stopping to ask information, he sees Pastorella and cannot leave. He manufactures conversation with the shepherds to avoid having to leave, and even this speech, though ostensibly aimed at the shepherds, is really meant for Pastorella:

> And euermore his speach he did apply
> To th' heards, but meant them to the damzels fantazy. (ix, 12)

Next he compounds his departure from dignity by becoming a shepherd and taking part in the rural pastimes, even wrestling, which we remember as a detail in Chaucer's burlesque of romance in the *Tale of Thopas*.

The possibility of the comic exploitation of disparity is always just below the surface in Book VI, because of the very nature of the book, its use of the romance conventions for the illustration of a social virtue. That is the probable reason why, though Book VI lacks extended comic passages of the size of the Hellenore episode in Book VI, it has perhaps more short comic passages than any other, places wherein the important personages of the story become for the moment ridiculous, as Calidore is in Arcady, or Serena, who when rescued by Calepine, will not speak for shame of her nakedness (viii, 50-51).

Picture and Dream

ONE OF THE OLDEST COMMONPLACES of Spenserian criticism emphasizes the pictorial quality of the *Faerie Queene*. It is customary to cite or mention the anecdote in which Pope reads the poem to a lady, who calls it a gallery of pictures. From that point the critics commonly take up the Horatian *ut pictura poesis* parallel which makes the graphic and the poetic arts sisters, compare specific passages with specific painters, most of whom were probably unknown to Spenser, and often complete the treatment by suggesting certain graphic conventions or pieces as sources for passages in the *Faerie Queene*.

The rebuttal is not so ancient, but seems also to have its own tradition. After all, calling a literary work a picture can have another implication, that it is artificial, removed from reality, of secondary inspiration rather than primary. Critics are not wanting who find Spenser's visual sense defective; these say that he does not see an object, but only a picture of an object, of which he in turn gives us a picture. These critics find Spenser's visual images artificial or confused.

It is usually rather easy to refute those who deny the visual quality to Spenser's descriptions by pointing out that such critics are requiring a representational kind of visualization, whereas Spenser's is dominantly abstract and stylized. It is, for instance, useless to ask what becomes of Una's lamb or how, if Redcross' horse was really pricking on the plain, Una's ass could keep up. Spenser does not follow the conventions of representational art or literature to which such questions are appropriate.

For the same reason, comparisons with Rubens, who was twenty when Spenser died, or with Mantegna and Botticelli, whose pictures Spenser probably never had a chance to see, do not help much in understanding Spenser's actual achievement. The *ut pictura poesis* parallel is an interesting historical study in ideas, but it has precious little to do with Spenser's practice. More helpful are studies which seek sources or parallels for descriptions and images in various arts and quasi-arts with which Spenser was acquainted: tapestry and arras, illuminations, emblems, heraldry, murals, and a multitude of artifacts. Most often such studies demonstrate how dependent is Spenser's visualization on the conventions of the art forms he knew.

In the middle ages the visual and literary arts were especially close. In fact, one of the principal tasks of both painting and sculpture was to illustrate literary texts, the Bible primarily, but also such profane texts as

Martianus Capella's *Marriage of Mercury* and the *Roman de la Rose*. It is not merely that the artist gets his initial inspiration from a literary text, which he then tries to translate into the appropriate expression of his art; literary sources supply him with a corpus of hieroglyphic symbols which is his main business to arrange into meaningful combinations, the keys of Peter, Synagoge's blindfold, the compasses of Geometry, and so on. These conventions were strong and they still survived in Spenser's time, not only in the more artistically deprived countries like England, but also in Italy itself. Neither Leonardo nor Michaelangelo dared break them: the one gives his Judas red hair and the other puts horns on his Moses.

Perhaps the real source of *ut pictura poesis* is not the epigram of Horace but the practice of the middle ages, in which the poet spends a great deal of his time describing mural paintings, tapestries, or windows while the artist devotes his labors to illustrating texts. This is the practice which Spenser was born into. It came to him from both sources. The immense treasury of ecclesiastical art painted on wall, graven in stone, and pictured in window was still largely untouched by Protestant zeal in his time. He had many opportunities to see illuminated manuscripts. Tapestries and arrases hung in every well-appointed home.

His master Chaucer inducted him into the poetic shorthand of describing scenes "wrought on the wal," as in the temples of Venus, Mars, and Diana in *The Knight's Tale;* "in the glasyinge ywroght," as the story of Troy in *The Book of the Duchess;* or graven in the wall like the scenes from the *Aeneid* in the *House of Fame*. This is the ambience, artistic and literary, in which Spenser worked. One of its important elements is that both artist and poet were often telling a story or making a point of morality. In an age when neither artist nor poet does these things the critic must never forget this identity of purpose.

Occasionally we can identify a detail in the *Faerie Queene* derived relatively unchanged from a pictorial source. In the episode of Mirabella the churlish Disdain with his black hair, turban, and iron club derives from the representation of "Daungier" in illuminated manuscripts of the *Roman de la Rose;* he is identical with Turpine's porter and Briana's seneschal, Maleffort.

The description of the three Graces on Mt. Acidale who

> two of them still froward seem'd to bee,
> But one still towards shew'd her selfe afore

repeats the traditional representation, both in ancient times and in the Renaissance (Botticelli, Raphael) and could easily derive from some pictorial representation. But, since Spenser moralizes it,

That good should from vs goe, then come in greater store (x, 24)

one suspects that a literary source, perhaps one of the mythographical treatises such as Natales Comes', lies behind the description.

An even more interesting example of the use of a pictorial motif is the scene in which Serena wandering away from Calepine and Calidore to pick flowers is bitten by the Blattant Beast. This is clearly based on the common medieval version of Orpheus and Euridice, in which Euridice is picking flowers when she is stung to death by a serpent, the moral interpretation of which is the deadly effect of carnal desire. An illustration in a manuscript of the famous *Ovide Moralisé* (Lyon 742, fol. 166^r) shows a dragon-like beast with legs, wings, and a curled tail, which could easily be the prototype of the Blattant Beast.

The moralization of pictures, or perhaps most accurately, the expression of moral meaning in picture, achieved its more complete expression in the emblem book, in which the hieroglyphic tendency of the middle ages achieved a form more medieval than anything found in the middle ages proper. The emblem book exerted a profound influence on Spenser, whose first publication was some translations from the verses in Van der Noodt's *Theater*, which is virtually an emblem book. Many motifs in Spenser's imagery and character description are paralleled in the emblem books. The ship in distress, which appears in Turpine's attack on Calepine (iv, 1) is a favorite of the emblematists, appearing in the works of Van der Noodt, Alciati, and Beza among others. Whitney's *Choice of Emblems*, the first English emblem book, has a picture of Hercules fighting the pigmies, who flock about him "like gnattes," a figure Spenser uses many times.

But it is only occasionally that Spenser's poetic use of a motif is sufficiently "pure" to establish a parallel in the emblem books. It is not the detail which is important, anyway, but the method. Spenser does not have to borrow his emblems; he can make up his own. Mirabella's bottle for tears and bag for "repentaunce for things past and gone" are completely in the emblem tradition.

Many of Spenser's emblematic creations occur in the processions and pageants which dot the *Faerie Queene;* the seven deadlies in the House of Pride (I, iv. 8-35); Caelia and her daughters in the House of Holiness (I, x, 4, 12-14, 29-31); the masque of Cupid in the House of Busirane (III, xii, 1-25). These are more numerous in the earlier books than in Book VI, where the Mirabella episode is the only example. This is conceived entirely as an emblematic procession, which is Spenser's adaptation of the quasi-theatrical pieces often produced in the fifteenth and sixteenth centuries as court masque, royal progress, pas d'armes, or civic spectacle.

Mirabella's entrance into the story is precisely in the manner of such a procession:

> A faire Mayden clad in mourning weed,
> Vpon a mangy iade vnmeetely set
> And a lewd foole her leading thorough dry and wet. (vi, 16)

Another commonplace of commentary on the *Faerie Queene* is that it has a dream-like quality. This arose perhaps even earlier than the cliche of the "gallery of pictures," being enunciated in 1650 by Davenant in his preface to *Gondibert*. Davenant considered dreaminess a defect as did most of the neo-classical critics. With the coming of romanticism it became a virtue and has remained so with the contemporary increase in concern with periconscious states. Close analysis, however, shows that "dream-like" or "dreamy" comprehends several phenomena, some of them not even related. The critics and commentators are not all talking about the same things; in a few instances the same critic is talking about two different things under the same name. It is well therefore to attempt a rude separation of the several meanings of the term.

Some critics are identifying the fairyland setting of the poem with the dream world. Fairyland is an externalization of the phenomena of dreams: both are the attainment of perfections unobtainable in consciousness. Perhaps they are thinking of day dreams, fantasies, wish fulfillment. Of this last there is ample in the *Faerie Queene*, though I believe it dominates no book of the poem, least of all Book VI. But the Arcady into which Calidore rides after long and frustrating pursuit of the Blattant Beast is certainly wish fulfillment. Calidore wishes he could stop and rest, and lo he is in the best of places to rest, among shepherds who know no evil, with a wise old man for counsel and a rural goddess for worship. Up to Mount Acidale, Calidore's sojourn in Arcady is the rearrangement of the world to suit wish rather than experience.

From Mount Acidale onward it is a different sort of dream, the kind in which the dreamer is frustrated. Calidore sees the vision of perfect grace, but only for an instant. Just as he advances to seize it, the vision vanishes. This is the practice of fairies when they are spied on, but it is also the end of many a dream. What happens on Mount Acidale is repeated in Arcady. Calidore has won Pastorella; then he returns from hunting one day to find that all of Arcady has been taken off by the Brigands. This is the nearest approach of Book VI to the dream of terror, the nightmare, so apparent in the monsters of other parts of the *Faerie Queene*.

Some of the effect of the *Faerie Queene* must surely be explainable by the models which Spenser used. A large part of the literature of the fourteenth century belongs to the dream-vision genre. Chaucer, whom

Spenser called master, was a notable practitioner of this genre, as was also Langland. The dream vision is par excellence the medieval form developed for the exploration of the psyche and for the treatment of morality, both large items in Spenser's practice.

Readers of dream visions soon get used to the experience of finding themselves somewhere, either spatially or topically, without knowing how they got there. Consider the beginning of the *Book of the Duchess*. After the Dreamer finally gets to sleep, we find ourselves in his chamber on a morning looking at scenes from the *Roman de la Rose* depicted on the walls. The sounds of a hunting party break up this experience and the dreamer joins the party:

> Took my hors, and forth I wente
> Oute of my chambre.

The reversal of the normal chronological order which produces the curious picture of the Dreamer mounting his horse while still in his chamber is doubtless intentional, for Chaucer is telling a dream. So too are the sudden appearance and disappearance of the hunting party, the whelp, the beasts of the woods and then "I was war of a man in blak." In a dream vision we don't have to be told what happened to the whelp, where the beasts went to, where the Man in Black came from.

This jumping from place to place, from detail to detail without any or with only a minimum of transition from one to another gives the reader the sensation of free association outside the normal frame of time and space. This is precisely the quality of dreams, which being products of the mind instead of the sensory apparatus, can abstract only the significant without bothering with the connective tissue of insignificance. Spenser manages his narrative in this manner. His is the narrative counterpart of the lack of perspective common to medieval pictorial art. The figures of a medieval mosaic are not standing on anything nor in front of anything. Though they may be solid enough in themselves they are free in space, not connected with other objects through intervening space. They have a separate existence of their own, and are not merely a separated part of all existence. They are abstracted and stylized.

Spenser produces this effect by his virtually unique handling of time and space. We have noted how space frequently serves for time in his narrative structure, but neither his time nor his space is external to the poem itself. The *Faerie Queene* contains no dates, neither season dates nor calendar dates. Except for the reference in the "Letter to Ralegh" to Gloriana's "annual feast," which is presumably Christmas, events in the *Faerie Queene* do not happen on Sunday, or Christmas, or the eighteenth day of April. "St. Valentide," when Cupid held his court, is the only such reference I can find in Book VI. There is only a rather fluid succession, in which a day or a night is the only unit. References to any time span longer than a day are very rare, numbering only three in Book VI.

To some extent sparseness of time reference is characteristic of Arthurian romance, a large part of which takes place in fairyland, where time does not obey earthly laws. Seasonal time, however, often plays a major role, since many of the stories are season myths in origin. Italian romance implies actual calendar time. Charlemagne is a historical figure and the First Crusade a historical event, and though the content of *Orlando Furioso* and *Girusalame Liberata* is largely mythic in origin, the reader never really forgets the historical frame of reference. Perhaps Arthur was a historical personage to some of Spenser's readers, but Spenser seems to be doing everything he can to free Arthur of any historicity.

(and liturgical)

If Spenser's use of time has some precedent in Arthurian romance, his use of space has none. Arthurian romance is partly laid in fairyland, but its heroes move out from and back to named geographical points, Camelot, Logres, Corbenic. Most of the places in Spenser are not named; they are a wood, a cave, a river. The few geographical names, Acidale, Arlo, Cleoplis, do not constitute points of reference from which one could construct a map of Spenser's fairyland, as you can of Ulysses' wanderings or even of Dante's Inferno.

It is impossible to overemphasize the affective effect of a system of temporal and spatial reference, even if it is fictional. It gives narrative a solidity and a credibility. Writers of ghost stories and similar exercises of fantasy know this well. They are always careful to build up a tissue of references to places and events locatable by map and calendar. I am much more disposed to believe that you actually saw a ghost if you say that it happened at the old house on the edge of town (with which I am quite familiar) as you were driving back from the dance at Centerville last Saturday night (which I can check).

Spenser's practice with time and space references is therefore the opposite of the expected, just as it is with characterization. He passes from the unfamiliar to the familiar, the universal to the concrete, the general to the specific. Generically, his practice is nearest to the personification allegory, as exemplified by pieces like the *Roman de la Rose*, DeGuilleville's pilgrimages, and the moral plays. The prime function of such pieces is to give literary expression to experiences of the conscious and unconscious, both collective and individual. It is necessarily abstract and non-representational.

But in a curious way it has a truth to experience lacking in the more intelligible and representational modes. It is the search after this kind of truth that led Freud and his followers to the serious study of dreams. In fact, the experience of an individual caught up in an action too large or rapid for his simultaneous comprehension—a soldier in a battle—is dream-like. If one compares the account of Waterloo in Hugo's *Les Miserables* with that of Caporetto in Hemingway's *Farewell to Arms* the difference becomes clear. Hugo is writing history, a rational, intelligible account from a point of view long after and far above the action; Hemingway is seeing the action from the point of view of a participant. We have noted that Spenser, by design or accident, often does adopt a very limited point of view. So he achieves an individual experience, not anchored in time and space, and hence having the qualities we often ascribe to dreams.

Conclusion

THE LAST COMPLETE book of the *Faerie Queene* lacks many of the features often regarded as characteristic of Spenser, even some described as necessary to the romance genre. It contains little in the way of marvels and magic, which the well-known description of Frye lists as specific to romance. Except for the epiphany on Mount Acidale and the Salvage Man's invulnerability, the story manages without magic or supernatural interventions. It has no clear example of the demonic or the monstrous, for the Blattant Beast, despite its hellish ancestry, turns out to be not much more dangerous than a dog or a steer. Book VI is also comparatively deficient in personification allegory, only the episode of Mirabella and Timias' encounter with Despetto, Defetto, and Decetto employing the technique of personification. Similarly with myth. The ancestry of the Blattant Beast and the scene on Mount Acidale are the only samples.

The reason for the comparative lack of personification and myth, of the elements which earlier commentators have taken as the very essence of "allegory," is the theme. Courtesy is a lowly virtue, without spiritual exhaltation or demonic opposition. It flourishes in a middle earth between heaven and hell, and its champions as well as its opponents are human. Perhaps the most important literary effect of this absence of both malign and benign magic and of the de-emphasis of the most visible bearers of allegory is the emergence into full importance of the narrative mode and pattern. Though present throughout the *Faerie Queene*, the narrative technique is often obscured by marvels, magic, and thematic intent. More than in any other book, the narrative has to carry the meaning of Book VI.

This in Spenser's practiced hands it is quite capable of doing. We have become so used to this manner of narrative from the romances and novels of succeeding centuries that we often forget, as C. S. Lewis reminds us, how new it was in Spenser's time, in fact, that he was really the first complete practitioner. The interwoven lines and the interlaced motifs find precedents in the vulgate romances and especially in the Italians. But the joining of such a structure with serious thematic content, the experiments in technical subtleties such as point of view, exposition and the creation of suspense—these are largely Spenser's own achievement.

In the *Faerie Queene* itself we can trace the development of this new narrative technique. The first two books are self-contained units. In them a steel frame of theme supports the narrative. Book III abandons the one-line thematic development, and the narrative structure almost collapses. It takes about half of Book IV to straighten up all the lines of narrative left tangled at the end. Book V is substantially a return to the method of the first two, a one book unit with the narrative line firmly controlled by thematic purposes. But Book VI solves the problem of how to write a book which, while composing a unit, still is continuous in the sense that it sets up narrative lines for future exploitation.

The solution is to make the quest of the champion a frame which encloses the many-branching lines of the middle section. Every plot line of Book VI reaches its natural denouement: Serena and Pastorella are rescued; Turpine is punished; Timias delivered; the Blattant Beast chained. Nevertheless, like a skilled billiards player, Spenser is in perfect position for the next shot. Arthur, Timias, Enias, and Salvage ride off into a further adventure; Calepine has rescued Serena but not wed her; so with Calidore and Pastorella. And even the Blattant Beast is loose again at the end of the book.

The narrative certainly carries the theme. It is even fair to say that narrative dominates theme, if we mean that narrative line and pattern is more visible than thematic purpose. The lazy or naive reader might even fail to notice that the story carries out the author's purpose to exemplify courtesy in both its practice and its malpractice.

To accomplish his analysis of Courtesy Spenser employs three means: a thematic line mainly coincident with the narrative line, and needing little in the way of commentary to help it along; a practice of giving personages names which, while not personifications, still serve to cue the reader to the thematic function of the personage; and the structural use of certain large-scale metaphors which I have called "premises" to support the narrative and so make it thematically functional.

The incidents and episodes which compose the thematic as well as the narrative line are brilliantly conceived to exemplify courtesy and discourtesy: Briana's selfishness and Turpine's rudeness contrasted with Calidore's willingness to sacrifice both effort and dignity to help anyone in trouble. The exemplification of courtesy or discourtesy is underlined by the names of the personages. Courtesy is a beautiful gift, and that is the meaning of the name of its chief proponent, Calidore.

Narrative and theme operate in a supporting framework of the premises that ancient times were more virtuous than modern ones, that virtue is characteristic of gentle blood, and the quasi-premise that the perfect image of behavior is to be found in knights questing in fairyland. These are all figures, images, not literal reports, for on close inspection, one perceives, for instance, that it is not gentility that produces virtue, but virtue which is a proof of gentility. Most premises are balanced with anti-premises, which together lead into the inner meaning.

The effect of balance and stability is also characteristic of the texture of this last complete book of the *Faerie Queene*. At first sight it would appear to be thin in rhetorical pattern and in imagery. Verse after verse only tells what happened in the baldest, least decorated, most literal language. Partially this is an effect of the dominance of narrative. Heavily patterned verse thick with images, though perhaps desirable in compressed lyric utterance, is fatal to narrative, as the practice of Donne proves.

The normal practice of Spenser is to establish a balance by the equality of opposites. The tendency of stanzaic verse to break into discrete units he neutralizes by so using his stanza as to produce effects of continuity and fluency. The result is a rather plain style, self-effacing so as to let the narrative line show through. At the climax of a narrative development, however, this plain style thickens into a passage of high tension and excitement, as in the sacrifice of Serena. Such scenes, of which there are only three or four in the book, are the more mature equivalents of the "set pieces" of the earlier books, most of them pageants such as the parade of the Seven Deadlies at the House of Pride in Book I. Book VI has no set pieces, only heightened episodes in the narrative.

One could call Book VI the most comic in the *Faerie Queene*. True, it lacks both explicitly comic characters like Braggadocchio and obviously funny episodes like the elopement of Hellenore and Paridell, but the whole of the book is capable of being interpreted as comic. The villains, Briana and Turpine, even the Cannibals and the Brigands, are not such monsters that we cannot be amused at their selfishness, vanity, and cowardice. The book abounds in the incongruous, Briana accusing Calidore of discourtesy, Calepine and the squalling infant, the scratchings and bitings of the Blattant Beast when Calidore finally bays it.

The apparent thinness of explicit and formal imagery ought not to blind us to the range of affective mechanisms, especially of the pictorial quality, which the book shares with all of Spenser's work. It is sometimes possible to find a specific graphic symbol, notably in the emblem books, which inspired Spenser. Of far greater significance, however, is Spenser's practice of making his own pictorial arrangements, rather than borrowing them from the common stock.

The peculiar quality of Spenser's pictorial imagination is sometimes said to be dream-like. The most notable examples of this quality are not to be found in Book VI, neither the fantasies of wish fulfillment like the vision of the fleeing Florimell, nor the nightmares of terror like the cave of Mammon. But if a clarity and detachment of image, a suspension of time and place, a substitution of unconscious association for conscious logic are marks of the dream, these are present in this as in all other books of the *Faerie Queene*.

CONCLUSION

However, it would hardly be appropriate to cast the treatment of courtesy in the form of a dream. The corner of fairyland through which Calidore pursues the Blattant Beast lies very close to the world of actuality, and the lives of its denizens have been greatly modified by the mere mortals who dwell just across its border.

DOCUMENTATION

p. 3 I have not found much critical discussion of Spenser's narrative technique. John Arthos, *On the Poetry of Spenser and the Form of Romances* (London: Allen and Unwin, 1956), touches on narrative in many places, particularly in "The Romantic Scene," pp. 40-64, but is interested more in theme and affect than in pure narrative pattern. The best description of the interlaced, tapestry-like narrative of Arthurian romance is in Eugene Vinaver's edition of Malory: *The Works of Sir Thomas Malory* (Oxford, 1947), I, xlviii-lviii. The best general treatment of narrative I have found is Wayne C. Booth, *The Rhetoric of Fiction* (University of Chicago, 1961), from which I have received many helpful suggestions.

p. 20 Booth, especially the section "True Novels Must Be Realistic" characterizes the overemphasis on "showing" rather than "telling" as a "crippling dogma."

p. 27 Harry Berger, Jr., "A Secret Discipline," in *Form and Convention in the Poetry of Edmund Spenser*, ed. William Nelson (English Institute Papers, New York, 1961), p. 39, also makes the point that Spenser repeats his motifs, but he finds that the second occurrence is "always worse or more ineffective than the first." I do not find this. In fact, the rescue of Pastorella seems an augmentation and elaboration of the rescue of Serena.

p. 29 This description of romance occurs in Northrop Frye, *Anatomy of Criticism* (Princeton, 1957), p. 33. I use his modes throughout this section.

p. 30 On the variability of time in fairyland see Howard Patch, *The Other World* (Harvard, 1950), especially p. 58.

p. 34 The moralizing of classical mythology, which certainly began in the Hellenistic period, if not before, reached perhaps its greatest height in the sixteenth century in the work of the mythographers such as Lilio Giraldi and Natale Conti (Natalis Comes). Concerning this phenomenon and its importance see Douglas Bush, *Mythology and the Renaissance Tradition in English Poetry* (revised edition: New York: Norton, 1963), especially pp. 28-30, 69-73; Jean Seznec, *The Survival of the Pagan Gods*, translated by Barbara F. Sessions (New York: Harper Torchbooks, 1961), especially pp. 219-256; Henry G. Lotspeich, *Classical Mythology in the Poetry of Edmund Spenser* (Princeton Studies in English no. 9, 1932).

p. 35 An interesting example of the analogy between physician and confessor is the sermon of Richard Helmslay, O. P. ca. 1379 reported in W. A. Pantin, *The English Church in the Fourteenth Century* (Cambridge University Press, 1955), pp. 164-165.

p. 35 The register of Hamo of Hythe, Bishop of Rochester, 1319-52 preserves records of many morals cases adjudicated in his court; *Registrum Hamonis Hythe Diocesis Roffensis*, ed. Charles Johnson (Oxford: Canterbury and York Society, 1948). In Spenser's day ecclesiastical courts were still functioning, though with reduced jurisdiction and prestige. Presumably memories of their former practices still persisted.

p. 36 For the speculations on the identification of Artegall and the other personages and incidents in the last canto of Book V see Josephine Waters Bennett, "The Allegory of Sir Artegall," *Studies in Philology*, XXXVII (1940), 177-200; also the summaries of Birch, Upton, Greenlaw, Gough, Jones, Schulze, and Heffner in the Variorum Spenser, V, 299-335.

p. 41 The paucity of scholarship and criticism on narrative technique is not duplicated with thematic meaning. The Variorum edition contains in the commentary on the text and in Appendices I, "The Plan and Conduct of Book VI," and II, "Sources," virtually all the important writing up to 1935. Important organized expositions of thematic meaning which I have found useful are: Janet Spens, *Spenser's Faerie Queene: An Interpretation* (London, 1934); C. S. Lewis, *The Allegory of Love* (Oxford, 1938), pp. 350-353; A. C. Hamilton, *The Structure of Allegory in the Faerie Queene* (Oxford, 1961), pp. 192-206. Mother Pauline Parker, *The Allegory of the Faerie Queene* (Oxford, 1960); Alastair Fowler, *Spenser and the Numbers of Time* (London, 1964), pp. 222-226; and Graham Hough, *A Preface to the Faerie Queene* (New York, 1963), pp. 201-212. I have borrowed from all of these, both positively, by adopting their explanations, and negatively, by finding it necessary to construct another explanation in reaction to one of theirs which I could not accept. Three special studies of significance were: H. C. Chang, *Allegory and Courtesy in Spenser* (Edinburgh, 1955); pp. 171-220; John L. Lievsay, *Stefano Guazzo and the English Renaissance* (Chapel Hill, 1960), especially pp. 96-99; and Harry Berger, Jr., "A Secret Discipline; The *Faerie Queene* Book VI," in *Form and Convention in the Poetry of Edmund Spenser*, ed. William Nelson (English Institute Essays, New York, 1961), pp. 35-75.

p. 47 Calepine's cowardice: Parker, p. 234, calls Calepine's situation "humiliation, even hiding behind Serena."

p. 49 The Cannibals: Parker, p. 245, and the comments on the passage in the Variorum.

p. 52 The platonic love of Timias and Belphebe: Isabel E. Rathborne, *The Meaning of Spenser's Fairyland* (New York, 1937), p. 220-221. Thomas P. Roche, Jr., *The Kindly Flame* (Princeton, 1964), pp. 136-148, takes this notion much farther: Belphebe "represents an aspect of Elizabeth, the virgin queen married to her kingdom."

p. 54 For a useful exploration of the implications of Spenser's practice in working out his thematic purpose in action see B. Nellish, "The Allegory of Guyon's Voyage: An Interpretation," *ELH*, XXX (1963), 89-106. Nellish finds that Spenser's "allegory" differs from the medieval "as noun differs from adverb." The Castle of Alma is nominal, Guyon's voyage adverbial. In Nellish's terminology most of Book VI is adverbial; only the flashback of the attack on Timias by Despetto, Decetto, and Defetto and the Mirabella episode is nominal.

p. 56 Melibee: I have not noted anyone who has indicated any other than a literal reading of Melibee's occupation at court. The Variorum comment on the passage (ix, 24) calls attention to a parallel in Tasso, and Judson, abstracted on p. 343, writes, typical of other commentators, "It is not, however, Coridon, the typical shepherd, who reveals true courtesy but rather Melibee, who had labored for ten years in the prince's garden."

p. 56 Calidore in Arcady: J. C. Maxwell, "The Truancy of Calidore," *ELH*, XIX (1952), 143-149, sees in Spenser's handling of Calidore's sojourn in Arcady a confusion between two antitheses, "quest vs. retirement" and "court vs. country."

A recent study agrees with me in rejecting the older notion that the Arcady episode is digressive or represents a dereliction by Calidore. Kathleen Williams, "Courtesy and Pastoral in *The Faerie Queene*, Book VI," *Review of English Studies*, XIII (1962), 337-346, argues that "the values which have been practically exemplified, both positively and negatively, in the stories of Serena, Turpine, Tristram, are here fully embodied, so that the pastoral interlude is not really an interlude at all, but the thematic centre which unifies the dispersed adventures preceding it." This is certainly true, but does not go quite far enough; it does not explain why Arcady must be destroyed.

p. 57 Epiphany: Northrop Frye, *Anatomy of Criticism*, pp. 61, 121, 203-206. Rathborne, p. 129, points out that canto x is the common place for the champion of the book to receive a vision: House of Holiness, Castle of Alma, Temple of Venus, etc.

R. F. Hill, "Colin Clout's Courtesy," *Modern Language Review*, LXVII (1962), 492-503, sees the vision on Mount Acidale as relevant only to Calidore's suit to Pastorella. Calidore has to perfect himself in courtesy to win her. This seems to me to invert the order of importance. Courtesy is the subject of Book VI. The wooing and winning of Pastorella, which requires Calidore to become a shepherd, is a means for perfecting his courtesy.

p. 59 Calidore's subterfuge: Duplicity in a good cause is a motif in the *Faerie Queene*. See Charles E. Mounts, "Virtuous Duplicity in the *Faerie Queene*," *Modern Language Quarterly*, VII (1946), 43-52. Other examples in Book VI are Calidore's story to Priscilla's parents and Enias' misrepresentation of Arthur's condition to Turpine.

p. 60 Spenser diminishes the Beast: Berger, "A Secret Discipline," p. 43.

p. 60 Calidore's insecure chaining: B. E. C. Davis in the Variorum, VI, p. 346.

p. 64 The three classical sources for etymologies were Sudias, *Lexicon* for Greek, Isidore of Seville, *Etymologiarum* for Latin, and St. Jerome, *De Nominibus Hebraicis* (Patrologia latina, xxiii) for Hebrew. The standard Greek dictionary of Spenser's time was Henricus Stephanus (Henri Estienne), *Thesaurus Graecae Linguae* (Paris, 1572-1573), from which directly or by second hand Spenser derived most or all of his knowledge of the meanings of Greek words. Thomas Cooper, *Thesaurus Linguae Romanae et Britannicae* (London, 1584), has a great deal of etymological information, Greek as well as Latin. Dewitt Starnes and Ernest William Talbert, *Classical Myth and Legend in Renaissance Dictionaries* (Chapel Hill, 1955), is an authoritative account of the sort of material, etymological and otherwise, to be found in dictionaries.

p. 68 The Blattant Beast: Leslie Hotson, "The Blatant Beast," *Studies in Honor of T. W. Baldwin* (Urbana, 1958), pp. 34-37. See also Lotspeich, p. 43. Merrit Y. Hughes, "Spenser's 'Blatant Beast'," *Modern Language Review*, XIII

(1918), 265-275, largely concerns the identification of the Beast with the Puritans made by Jonson in his *Conversations with Drummond*.

p. 68 Dragonopede: see note to p. 123 below.

p. 70 Calepine's name: For information on the dictionary of Calepine see Starnes and Talbert, pp. 3-4, 11-15. Also Parker, p. 223; Alice Blitch, *Etymon and Image in the Faerie Queene* (Michigan State Dissertation, 1965), pp. 220-23.

p. 70 Timias and Sir Walter Ralegh: See the Variorum, Appendix II, "The Prototype of Sir Calidore," pp. 349-364 for the various historical identifications, Sidney, Ralegh, Essex, etc.

pp. 71 Celtic fantasy in the Briana story: Edgar A. Hall, abstracted in the Variorum, pp. 365-367, offers several versions of the "castle of beards" story: in the Perlesvaus, Geoffrey of Monmouth, Suite Merline, Layamon's *Brut*, and Malory. Hall believes that Spenser knew the Perlesvaus version or an analogue of it.

p. 71 Sir Bruin: See Upton's note in the Variorum notes on this passage (iv, 33).

p. 71 Matilde: Blanchard, cited in the Variorum notes on this passage (iv, 29) sees a parallel between Spenser and Tasso which escapes me. The parallel, though not too immediate, between Spenser's Matilde and the mother of Henry II, who placed her son on the throne against great odds, seems stronger to me.

p. 71 Melissa: See Stephanus' *Thesaurus* under the respective words and Cooper's *Thesaurus* under "Melissa."

p. 72 Tristram: See Edgar A. Hall, "Spenser and the Old French Grail Romances," abstracted in the Variorum, pp. 367-371.

p. 72 Cannibals: The quote is from Pignafetta's account of Magellan in Hakluyt Society, LIII, 188; See also Ralegh's *Discovery of Guiana*, Hakluyt Society edition, p. 35.

p. 73 Mount Acidale: Besides Cooper's *Thesaurus*, see also Starnes and Talbert, pp. 81-82, who quote Servius on *Aeneid*, I, 720.

p. 73 Salvage Man: Richard Bernheimer, *Wild Men in the Middle Ages* (Harvard, 1952), especially chapters I and II, p. 113.

p. 75 Among recent writers using "image" for what I call "premise" are Roche, pp. 53-66, who writes, for instance of "the images of Britomart"; Graham Hough, pp. 105-111, where image is the opposite of theme; Hamilton, especially chapter V, "This Antique Image"; Lyle Glazier, *Spenser's Imagery of Good and Evil in the Faerie Queene* (Harvard Dissertation, 1950); Paul J. Alpers, *Narrative and Rhetoric in the Faerie Queene* (Harvard Dissertation, 1959).

p. 76 Hough, pp. 129-130, presents a good recent appraisal of "historical allegory," though I would subtract from his examples the Timias-Belphebe story, which I do not believe had anything to do with the Ralegh-Throgmorton affair.

p. 77 "Timeless, wavering myth" is from Robert Graves, *Hercules My Shipmate* (Grosset Universal Library—original edition 1945), p. 152.

p. 78 Gentility: William Nelson, *The Poetry of Edmund Spenser* (New

York, 1963), pp. 278-281, points out that gentility is really a metaphor, not a literal statement.

p. 79 Nature and Art: Lewis, *Allegory of Love*, pp. 323-333. See also Millar MacClure, "Nature and Art in the *Faerie Queene*," *ELH*, XXVIII (1961), 1-20. Where MacClure sees ambiguities and contradictions in Spenser's notions of nature and art, I see premise and anti-premise.

p. 82 Cult of Arthurianism: Charles B. Millican, *Spenser and the Table Round*, (Harvard, 1932), pp. 7-36, traces the use of the Arthurian legend for nationalistic propaganda by Henry VII and his successors, pp. 37-105 showing the existence of a "round table" in the reign of Elizabeth.

p. 83 Fairyland: The most complete study of Spenser's fairyland is Rathborne's *Meaning of Spenser's Fairyland*, already cited. Roche, pp. 33-50, suggests implications for the treatment of space and time.

p. 87 Dream-like quality: Most recently in Hough, *Preface to the Faerie Queene*, pp. 96-98.

p. 89 Colloquial: A good description of the parataxis of colloquial language is found in Otto Jespersen, *Language* (London, 1922) pp. 251-252.

p. 90 The text used for Donne is *The Complete Poetry and Selected Prose of John Donne*, ed. Charles Coffin (New York, 1952).

p. 92 Spenser's narrative style: C. S. Lewis has perhaps the most suggestive description of Spenser's narrative style, *English Literature in the Sixteenth Century* (Oxford, 1954), pp. 389-392. One statement is especially apt: "In an age when poetry was soon to be almost too poetical, he kept open the great thoroughfare of verse for long-distance travellers in workday clothes."

p. 92 Metaphor and letter: The largest collection of such confusions with the most astringent comment on them is Paul J. Alpers, *Narrative and Rhetoric in the Faerie Queene* (Harvard Dissertation, 1958).

p. 92 Archaism: On the question of Spenser's archaism critics of the last forty years have been less sure than their predecessors, doubtless because increased knowledge of the development of the language made it more difficult to confuse the usage of Spenser's own day with that of the critic's. Some sample treatments are W. L. Renwick, *Edmund Spenser* (London, 1925), pp. 77-96, containing a valuable summary of critical theory and poetic practice, particularly of the Pléade, which might have influenced Spenser; H. S. V. Jones, *A Spenser Handbook* (New York, 1930), who cites Roscoe Parker, "Spenser's Language and the Pastoral Tradition," *Language*, I, no. 3 (1925), 80-87, who finds the "percentage" of archaisms in *Colin Clout's Come Home Again* to be .81 as compared with 3.19 for the February Eclogue of the *Shepherds Calendar;* and W. S. B. Watkins, *Shakespeare and Spenser* (Boar's Head edition, 1961, original edition, 1950), pp. 264-270, who emphasizes Spenser's discipleship to Chaucer. I have not found any discussion of language in the most recent critics.

p. 94 Spenserian stanza: The only thorough study of the versification of Spenser is Frederic Reeve, *The Stanza of the Faerie Queene* (Princeton Dissertation, 1942), to which may be added the perceptive comments, primarily on other works than the *Faerie Queene*, of Watkins, pp. 269-279 and three special studies on continuity: Tucker Brooke, "Stanza Connection in the *Faerie*

Queene," Modern Language Notes, XXXVII (1922), 223-227; Arnold Stein, "Stanza Continuity in the *Fairie Queene," Modern Language Notes,* LIX (1944), 114-118; and R. J. Schoeck, "Alliteration as a Means of Stanza Connection in the *Faerie Queene," Modern Language Notes,* LXIV (1949), 90-93.

p. 99 Among the many treatments of Spenser's imagery, I have profited most from Rosamond Tuve, *Elizabethan and Metaphysical Imagery;* Lyle Glazier, *Spenser's Imagery;* Judith Dundas, *The Imagery of Spenser's Faerie Queene* (University of Wisconsin Dissertation, 1957); and a series of articles by Grace Landrum, *Shakespeare Association Bulletin,* XI (1936), 142-148; XVI (1941), 89-101, 131-139; XVII (1942), 190-199; XVIII (1943), 22-29; *ELH,* VIII (1941), 198-213.

p. 99 "Two other sorts of images": This distinction corresponds roughly to Glazier's into primary (simple metaphor or simile) and secondary (fabric-making), though Glazier would include as secondary what I call premise.

p. 105 Bagpipe: For the tradition see Edward A. Black, "Chaucer's Millers and Their Bagpipes," *Speculum,* XXIX (1954), 239-242; D. W. Robertson, Jr., *Preface to Chaucer* (Princeton, 1963), p. 243. An emblem drawn by Theodore Galle in Jan David, *Occasio Arrepta,* (Antwerp, 1605), p. 29, under the legend "Stimulante daemone, misere eluditur Occasio," shows a boyish, winged, tailed, and goat-legged demon playing a bagpipe. John Friedman provided me this reference.

p. 105 Bodily health as a metaphor: See note on p. 35, also Chaucer's *Summoner's Tale,* ll. 1817, 1892, 1956.

p. 105 Glazier, *Spenser's Imagery,* pp. 400-401; Paul J. Alpers, *Narrative and Rhetoric in the Faerie Queene* (Harvard Dissertation, 1959), pp. 28-112, analyzes several passages which seem to exhibit a disparity between thematic intention and metaphor. Most of the analyses seem to me nit-picking, but on the healing of Serena and Timias he is undoubtedly right.

p. 107 "Intellectual tightrope": Glazier, "The Nature of Spenser's Imagery," *Modern Language Quarterly,* XVI (1955), p. 307.

p. 108 Purgatory of Dames: Nelson cited in the Variorum comments on vii, 32-37. The material cited from E. B. Fowler, *Spenser and the Courts of Love,* is also pertinent.

p. 108 Penances: The register of Hamo of Hythe, cited previously, preserves many examples of penances for such offenses as fornication, adultery, breaking of a vow of chastity.

p. 110 Song of Songs: Barroway, abstracted in the Variorum comments on viii, 42, first noticed the source of this imagery.

p. 113 "One of Spenser's few consciously humorous passages": The Variorum comments on iv, 21, in which the bear finds the rock Calepine has thrust into his mouth a bit indigestible. The only organized discussions of Spenser's humor I have found are Charles B. Burke, "The 'Sage and Serious' Spenser," *Notes and Queries,* CLXXV (1938), 457-458; Watkins, "Spenser's High Comedy" pp. 293-304; Allen H. Gilbert, "Spenser's Comedy," *Tennessee Studies in Literature,* II (1957), 95-104; Robert O. Evans, "Spenserian Humor; *Faerie Queene* III and IV," *Neuphilologische Mitteilungen,* LX (1959), 288-299. Gilbert, who inherited Burke's unfinished study of Spenserian comedy, furnishes a very useful list of passages.

p. 115 *Nun's Priest's Tale:* Mortimer J. Donovan, "The Moralitee of the Nun's Priest's Tale," *Journal of English and Germanic Philology,* LII (1953), 498-508; Robertson, pp. 274, 351-52, 367, 376.

p. 121 Spenser and the artists: The story of Pope's elderly lady is in Joseph Spence, *Anecdotes,* ed. Samuel W. Singer (2nd edition, London, 1858), pp. 224-225. For recent examples of comparing Spenser's descriptions with specific painters see Watkins, pp. 235-243; and Jean Hagstrum, *The Sister Arts,* (Chicago, 1958), pp. 76-77.

p. 121 Spenser's visual sense defective: Three attacks on Spenser's visual sense are Jefferson Fletcher, "The Painter of the Poets," *Studies in Philology,* XIV (1917), 164-165; Rudolf Gottfried, "The Pictorial Element in Spenser's Poetry," *ELH,* XIX (1952), 203-213; and Alpers, the whole of chapter II. Gottfried drew an answer from Carl Robinson Sonn, "Spenser's Imagery," *ELH,* XXVI (1959), 156-170.

p. 121 *Ut pictura:* The most complete study of this parallel is William Hoyt Carter, Jr., *Ut Pictura Poesis* (Harvard Dissertation, 1948). Carter, pp. 149-153, reviews the state of art in England in Spenser's time. He refers to the Lumly and the Earl of Leicester's collections. The inventory of the latter is printed by William J. Thoms, *Notes and Queries,* Series 3, II, (1862), 201-202, 224-226. Most of the pictures seem to be portraits; some are mythological subjects. Spenser may have had an opportunity to see such collections before he left for Ireland or on his visits back, but one can hardly suppose they would have left very lasting impressions. Graham Hough, "Spenser and Renaissance Iconography," *Essays in Criticism,* XI (1961), 233-235, makes the valuable point that Spenser, though "working entirely in the spirit of the art of his time," is not necessarily drawing his icons from a common stock.

p. 122 Hieroglyphic symbols: This term is that of Emile Male, *The Gothic Image* (Harper Torchbook, 1958; originally published, 1913), p. 2.

p. 122 Descriptions of paintings, etc: See, for instance, D. W. Robertson, pp. 242, 257-258.

p. 122 Illuminated MSS: Tuve, "Spenser and Some Pictorial Conventions," pp. 150-154.

p. 122 Daungier: The same, pp. 166-167.

p. 123 I am indebted to John Friedman for this reference. His unpublished Michigan State University thesis contains a complete account of this version of the Orpheus and Euridice legend, pp. 231-281. Plate IV has the illustration as well as a rather similar one from another manuscript of the *Ovide Moralisé,* Bibliothèque Nationale, Fr. 871, fol. 196^r.

p. 123 Emblem Books: Two dissertations study Spenser's use of the emblem books: Sister Mary Louise Beutner, A. M. S. L., *Spenser and the Emblem Writers* (St. Louis University Dissertation, 1941); and Jack W. Jessee, *Spenser and the Emblem Books* (University of Kentucky Dissertation, 1955). Sister Mary Louise discovers several uses of pre-existing emblems: the ship in distress, 141-143 (Van der Noot), 241-242 (Theodore de Bèze); other epic similes, 138-153; Hercules and the gnats, 259-260. Jessee is more concerned with Spenser's use of the method to create his own emblems, pp. v-vii.

p. 124 Dream-like quality: Three recent critics who treat the dream-like quality of Spenser are C. S. Lewis, *English Literature*, p. 387, who suggests that the clarity of Spenser's descriptions suggests a dream; Hough, *Preface*, pp. 131-137, who uses the work of Freud in a "suggestive rather than exhaustive" consideration; and Judith Dundas, who traces the history of the notion and identifies lack of logical, as against symbolic, coherence as the main manifestation of dream-like quality. Charles G. Osgood, *Poetry as a Means of Grace* (Princeton, 1941), p. 69 denies the notion entirely: "We find it no dream world, no 'escape' world so much sought by the moderns," but the phrasing suggests that he is using the term in a different sense.

p. 126 Time references: Jane Frank Allinson provided me with these time references in the *Faerie Queene*. The three in Book VI are vii, 38 (Mirabella's *two years* of wandering); ii, 30 (Tristram has lived in the land since he was *ten years old*); and ix, 25 (Melibee's *ten years* as a gardener).

p. 126 Time and space in Italian Romance: Hough, *Preface*, p. 96, makes the point that Ariosto is full of geographical names (Scotland, Japan, Cathay), whereas Spenser has none.

Index

INDEX